∽IRISH∽
COOKING

Delicious recipes from pub fare to country classics

Publications International, Ltd.

Pictured on the front cover: Hearty Shepherd's Pie (*page 92*).
Pictured on the back cover (*clockwise from top*): Pub-Style Fish and Chips (*page 176*), Beef Barley Soup (*page 36*), and Corned Beef and Cabbage with Horseradish Mustard Sauce (*page 88*).
Pictured on the jacket flaps: Individual Beef Pot Pies (page 173), and Sautéed Garlic Potatoes (*page 158*).

ISBN: 978-1-4508-9107-3

Library of Congress Control Number: 2014938651

Manufactured in China.

8 7 6 5 4 3 2 1

Microwave Cooking: Microwave ovens vary in wattage. Use the cooking times as guidelines and check for doneness before adding more time.

CONTENTS

BREAKFAST

IRISH PORRIDGE WITH BERRY COMPOTE

4 cups plus 1 tablespoon water, divided
½ teaspoon salt
1 cup steel-cut oats
½ teaspoon ground cinnamon
⅓ cup half-and-half
¼ cup packed brown sugar
1 cup fresh strawberries, hulled and quartered
1 container (6 ounces) fresh blackberries
1 container (6 ounces) fresh blueberries
3 tablespoons granulated sugar

1. Bring 4 cups water and salt to a boil in medium saucepan over medium-high heat. Whisk in oats and cinnamon. Reduce heat to medium; simmer, uncovered, about 40 minutes or until water is absorbed and oats are tender. Remove from heat; stir in half-and-half and brown sugar.

2. Meanwhile, combine strawberries, blackberries, blueberries, granulated sugar and remaining 1 tablespoon water in small saucepan; bring to a simmer over medium heat. Cook 8 to 9 minutes or until berries are tender but still hold their shape, stirring occasionally.

3. Divide porridge among four bowls; top with berry compote.

Makes 4 servings

OATMEAL PECAN PANCAKES

1¼ to 1½ cups milk, divided
½ cup old-fashioned oats
⅔ cup all-purpose flour
⅓ cup whole wheat flour
2½ tablespoons packed brown sugar
2 teaspoons baking powder
½ teaspoon baking soda
¼ teaspoon salt
1 egg
2 tablespoons melted butter
½ cup chopped toasted pecans
Golden syrup, maple syrup and additional butter (optional)

1. Bring ½ cup milk to a simmer in small saucepan. Stir in oats. Remove from heat; let stand 10 minutes.

2. Combine all-purpose flour, whole wheat flour, brown sugar, baking powder, baking soda and salt in large bowl; mix well.

3. Combine egg and butter in medium bowl; mix well. Stir in oatmeal and ¾ cup milk. Add to flour mixture; stir just until blended. *Do not beat.* If mixture is too thick, thin with remaining ¼ cup milk, 1 tablespoon at a time. Stir in pecans.

4. Lightly grease large skillet or griddle; heat over medium heat. Pour batter into skillet by ¼ cupfuls; flatten slightly. Cook 2 minutes or until tops are bubbly and bottoms are golden brown. Turn and cook 2 minutes or until golden brown. Serve with golden syrup and additional butter, if desired.   *Makes 4 servings*

TIP: To toast pecans, spread in single layer in small heavy skillet. Cook and stir over medium heat 1 to 2 minutes, or until lightly browned. Remove from skillet immediately. Cool before using.

CARAMELIZED BACON

12 slices (about 12 ounces) applewood-smoked bacon
½ cup packed brown sugar
2 tablespoons water
¼ to ½ teaspoon ground red pepper

1. Preheat oven to 375°F. Line 15×10-inch jelly-roll pan with heavy-duty foil. Spray wire rack with nonstick cooking spray; place in prepared pan.

2. Cut bacon in half crosswise, if desired; arrange in single layer on prepared wire rack. Combine brown sugar, water and red pepper in small bowl; mix well. Brush generously over bacon.

3. Bake 20 to 25 minutes or until bacon is well browned. Immediately remove to serving platter; cool completely. *Makes 6 servings*

NOTE: Bacon can be prepared up to three days ahead and stored in the refrigerator between sheets of waxed paper in a resealable food storage bag. Let stand at room temperature at least 30 minutes before serving.

CHEDDAR AND LEEK STRATA

8 eggs
2 cups milk
½ cup porter or stout
2 cloves garlic, minced
¼ teaspoon salt
¼ teaspoon black pepper
1 loaf (16 ounces) sourdough bread, cut into ½-inch cubes
2 small leeks, coarsely chopped
1 red bell pepper, chopped
1½ cups (6 ounces) shredded Swiss cheese
1½ cups (6 ounces) shredded sharp Cheddar cheese

1. Spray 13×9-inch baking dish with nonstick cooking spray. Whisk eggs, milk, porter, garlic, salt and black pepper in large bowl until well blended.

2. Spread half of bread cubes in prepared baking dish. Sprinkle with half of leeks, half of bell pepper, ¾ cup Swiss cheese and ¾ cup Cheddar cheese. Repeat layers. Pour egg mixture evenly over top.

3. Cover tightly with plastic wrap or foil. Weigh top of strata down with slightly smaller baking dish. Refrigerate at least 2 hours or overnight.

4. Preheat oven to 350°F. Bake, uncovered, 40 to 45 minutes or until center is set. Serve immediately. *Makes 12 servings*

Apple Breakfast Cake

    3 cups all-purpose flour
    1 teaspoon baking soda
    1 teaspoon salt
    1 teaspoon ground cinnamon
    1 cup chopped walnuts
  1½ cups granulated sugar
    1 cup vegetable oil
    2 eggs
    2 teaspoons vanilla
    2 medium tart apples, peeled and chopped
      Powdered sugar

1. Preheat oven to 325°F. Spray 10-inch tube pan with nonstick cooking spray.

2. Sift flour, baking soda, salt and cinnamon into large bowl. Stir in walnuts. Combine granulated sugar, oil, eggs and vanilla in medium bowl; mix well. Stir in apples. Add to flour mixture; stir just until moistened. Spoon batter into prepared pan, spreading evenly.

3. Bake 1 hour or until toothpick inserted near center comes out clean. Cool in pan on wire rack 10 minutes. Loosen edge of cake, if necessary; remove to wire rack to cool completely.

4. Place cake on serving plate; sprinkle with powdered sugar just before serving.

Makes 12 servings

Bacon and Potato Quiche

1 refrigerated pie crust (half of 15-ounce package)
12 ounces thick-cut bacon, cut crosswise into ½-inch pieces
½ medium onion, chopped
½ pound Yukon Gold potatoes, peeled and cut into ¼-inch dice
½ teaspoon chopped fresh thyme
1½ cups half-and-half
4 eggs
½ teaspoon *each* salt and black pepper
¾ cup (3 ounces) shredded Dubliner cheese
2 tablespoons chopped fresh chives

1. Preheat oven to 450°F. Line baking sheet with foil.

2. Roll out pie crust into 12-inch circle on floured surface. Line 9-inch pie plate with crust, pressing firmly against bottom and up side of plate. Trim crust to leave 1-inch overhang; fold under and flute edge. Prick bottom of crust with fork. Bake about 8 minutes or until crust is lightly browned. Remove to wire rack to cool slightly. *Reduce oven temperature to 375°F.*

3. Cook bacon in large skillet over medium heat about 10 minutes or until crisp, stirring occasionally. Drain on paper towel-lined plate. Drain all but 1 tablespoon drippings from skillet. Add onion, potatoes and thyme to skillet; cook about 10 minutes or until onion and potatoes are tender, stirring occasionally.

4. Place pie plate on prepared baking sheet. Whisk half-and-half, eggs, salt and pepper in medium bowl until well blended. Sprinkle cheese evenly over bottom of crust; top with onion mixture. Pour in egg mixture; sprinkle with chives.

5. Bake 35 to 40 minutes or until quiche is set and knife inserted into center comes out clean. Cool 10 minutes before slicing. *Makes 8 servings*

DATE-NUT GRANOLA

2 cups old-fashioned oats
2 cups barley flakes
1 cup sliced almonds
⅓ cup vegetable oil
⅓ cup honey
1 teaspoon vanilla
1 cup chopped dates

1. Preheat oven to 350°F. Spray 13×9-inch baking pan with nonstick cooking spray.

2. Combine oats, barley flakes and almonds in large bowl. Combine oil, honey and vanilla in small bowl; mix well. Pour honey mixture over oat mixture; stir until well blended. Pour into prepared pan.

3. Bake about 25 minutes or until toasted, stirring frequently after 10 minutes. Stir in dates while granola is still hot. Cool. Store tightly covered.

Makes 6 cups

Smoked Salmon and Spinach Frittata

2 tablespoons vegetable oil, divided
1 medium red onion, diced
1 clove garlic, minced
6 ounces baby spinach
10 eggs
1 teaspoon dried dill weed
¼ teaspoon salt
¼ teaspoon black pepper
4 ounces smoked salmon, chopped
4 ounces Dubliner cheese, cut into ¼-inch cubes

1. Position oven rack in upper-middle position. Preheat broiler.

2. Heat 1 tablespoon oil in large ovenproof nonstick skillet. Add onion; cook 7 to 8 minutes or until softened, stirring occasionally. Add garlic; cook and stir 1 minute. Add spinach; cook 3 minutes or just until wilted. Transfer mixture to small bowl.

3. Whisk eggs, dill, salt and pepper in large bowl until blended. Stir in salmon, cheese and spinach mixture.

4. Heat remaining 1 tablespoon oil in same skillet over medium heat. Add egg mixture; cook about 3 minutes, stirring gently to form large curds. Cook without stirring 5 minutes or until eggs are just beginning to set.

5. Transfer skillet to oven. Broil 2 to 3 minutes or until frittata is puffed, set and lightly browned. Let stand 5 minutes; carefully slide frittata onto large plate or cutting board. Cut into wedges. *Makes 6 to 8 servings*

Corned Beef Hash

2 large russet potatoes, peeled and cut into ½-inch cubes
½ teaspoon salt
¼ teaspoon black pepper
¼ cup (½ stick) butter
1 cup chopped onion
½ pound corned beef, finely chopped
1 tablespoon horseradish
4 eggs

1. Place potatoes in large skillet; add water to cover. Bring to a boil over high heat. Reduce heat to low; simmer 6 minutes. (Potatoes will be firm.) Remove potatoes from skillet; drain well. Sprinkle with salt and pepper.

2. Melt butter in same skillet over medium heat. Add onion; cook and stir 5 minutes. Stir in corned beef, horseradish and potatoes; mix well. Press mixture with spatula to flatten.

3. Reduce heat to low; cook 10 to 15 minutes. Turn hash in large pieces; pat down and cook 10 to 15 minutes or until bottom is well browned.

4. Meanwhile, bring 1 inch of water to a simmer in small saucepan. Break 1 egg into shallow dish; carefully slide into water. Cook 5 minutes or until white is opaque. Remove with slotted spoon to plate; keep warm. Repeat with remaining eggs.

5. Top each serving of hash with 1 egg. Serve immediately.   *Makes 4 servings*

Broccoli, Potato and Bacon Egg Pie with Cheddar Cheese

2 cups cooked broccoli florets

1½ cups cooked diced potatoes (about 2 medium)

1½ cups (lightly packed) grated CABOT® Sharp Cheddar Cheese (about 6 ounces)

4 slices cooked bacon, chopped

1 unbaked 9-inch deep-dish or 10-inch pie shell

6 large eggs

2 large egg yolks

1½ cups heavy cream

1 teaspoon mild paprika

½ teaspoon salt

¼ teaspoon freshly ground black pepper

1. Preheat oven to 350°F.

2. Distribute broccoli, potatoes, cheese and bacon evenly in pie shell. In mixing bowl, whisk together whole eggs and egg yolks until well combined; add cream, paprika, salt and pepper and whisk again.

3. Pour cream mixture evenly over ingredients in pie shell. Bake for 30 to 40 minutes or until golden on top and set all the way to center.

Makes 6 to 8 servings

Irish Whiskey Cured Salmon

1 skin-on salmon fillet (1¾ pounds), pin bones removed
2 tablespoons Irish whiskey
⅓ cup packed dark brown sugar
3 tablespoons salt
   Black bread or Irish soda bread (optional)
   Fresh dill, crème fraîche, thinly sliced red onion and/or capers (optional)

1. Line rimmed baking sheet with plastic wrap. Rinse salmon and pat dry with paper towels. Arrange salmon, skin side down, on prepared baking sheet; brush with whiskey.

2. Combine brown sugar and salt in small bowl; rub mixture over salmon. Wrap plastic wrap securely around salmon. Top with another sheet of plastic wrap.

3. Place second baking sheet on top of salmon, then place heavy skillet or several cans on top to weigh it down. Refrigerate salmon at least 48 hours and up to 72 hours.

4. Remove top baking sheet. Unwrap salmon and rinse under cold water to remove any remaining salt mixture. Pat dry with paper towels. Cut salmon into very thin slices; serve with bread and assorted toppings, if desired. Refrigerate leftover salmon up to 2 days.   *Makes 6 to 8 servings*

TIP: Ask your fishmonger to remove the pin bones when purchasing the salmon. (Often this is already done, or you can remove the pin bones at home with tweezers.)

SOUPS

PORK AND CABBAGE SOUP

8 ounces pork loin, cut into ½-inch cubes
1 medium onion, chopped
2 slices bacon, finely chopped
2 cups reduced-sodium beef broth
2 cups reduced-sodium chicken broth
1 can (about 28 ounces) whole tomatoes, drained and coarsely chopped
2 medium carrots, sliced
¾ teaspoon dried marjoram
1 bay leaf
1 teaspoon salt
⅛ teaspoon black pepper
¼ medium cabbage, chopped
2 tablespoons chopped fresh parsley

1. Heat large saucepan or Dutch oven over medium heat. Add pork, onion and bacon; cook and stir until pork is no longer pink and onion is crisp-tender. Drain fat.

2. Stir in broth, tomatoes, carrots, marjoram, bay leaf, salt and pepper; bring to a boil over high heat. Reduce heat to medium-low; simmer, uncovered, about 30 minutes. Remove and discard bay leaf. Skim off fat.

3. Add cabbage; bring to a boil over high heat. Reduce heat to medium-low; simmer, uncovered, about 15 minutes or until cabbage is tender. Stir in parsley.

Makes 6 servings

Chicken, Barley and Vegetable Soup

8 ounces boneless skinless chicken breasts, cut into ½-inch pieces
8 ounces boneless skinless chicken thighs, cut into ½-inch pieces
¾ teaspoon salt
¼ teaspoon black pepper
1 tablespoon olive oil
½ cup uncooked pearl barley
4 cans (about 14 ounces each) reduced-sodium chicken broth
2 cups water
1 bay leaf
2 cups whole baby carrots
2 cups diced peeled potatoes
2 cups sliced mushrooms
2 cups frozen peas
3 tablespoons sour cream
1 tablespoon chopped fresh dill *or* 1 teaspoon dried dill weed

1. Sprinkle chicken with salt and pepper. Heat oil in large saucepan or Dutch oven over medium-high heat. Add chicken; cook without stirring 2 minutes or until golden. Turn chicken; cook 2 minutes. Remove chicken to plate.

2. Add barley to saucepan; cook and stir 2 minutes or until barley starts to brown, adding 1 tablespoon broth if needed to prevent burning. Add remaining broth, water and bay leaf; bring to a boil. Reduce heat to low; cover and simmer 30 minutes.

3. Add chicken, carrots, potatoes and mushrooms; cook 10 minutes or until vegetables are tender. Add peas; cook 2 minutes. Remove and discard bay leaf.

4. Top with sour cream and dill; serve immediately.   *Makes 6 servings*

POTATO AND LEEK SOUP

4 cups chicken broth

3 potatoes, peeled and diced

1½ cups chopped cabbage

1 leek, diced

1 onion, chopped

2 carrots, diced

1 teaspoon salt

½ teaspoon caraway seeds

½ teaspoon black pepper

1 bay leaf

½ cup sour cream

1 pound bacon, cooked and crumbled

¼ cup chopped fresh parsley

SLOW COOKER DIRECTIONS

1. Combine broth, potatoes, cabbage, leek, onion, carrots, salt, caraway seeds, pepper and bay leaf in slow cooker; mix well.

2. Cover; cook on LOW 8 to 10 hours or on HIGH 4 to 5 hours.

3. Remove and discard bay leaf. Combine ½ cup hot liquid from slow cooker and sour cream in small bowl; mix well. Add sour cream mixture and bacon to slow cooker; stir until well blended. Sprinkle with parsley.   *Makes 6 to 8 servings*

CURRIED PARSNIP SOUP

3 pounds parsnips, peeled and cut into 2-inch pieces
1 tablespoon olive oil
2 tablespoons butter
1 medium yellow onion, chopped
2 stalks celery, diced
3 cloves garlic, minced
1 tablespoon salt
1 to 2 teaspoons curry powder
½ teaspoon grated fresh ginger
½ teaspoon black pepper
8 cups reduced-sodium chicken broth
    Toasted bread slices (optional)
    Chopped fresh chives (optional)

1. Preheat oven to 400°F. Line large baking sheet with foil.

2. Combine parsnips and oil in large bowl; toss to coat. Spread in single layer on prepared baking sheet. Bake 35 to 45 minutes or until parsnips are tender and lightly browned around edges, stirring once halfway through cooking.

3. Meanwhile, melt butter in large saucepan or Dutch oven over medium heat. Add onion and celery; cook and stir about 8 minutes or until vegetables are tender and onion is translucent. Add garlic, salt, curry powder, ginger and pepper; cook and stir 1 minute. Add parsnips and broth; bring to a boil over medium-high heat. Reduce heat to medium-low; cover and simmer 10 minutes.

4. Working in batches, blend soup in blender or food processor until smooth. Transfer blended soup to large bowl. Serve with toasted bread, if desired; garnish with chives. *Makes 6 to 8 servings*

Mushroom Soup

6 tablespoons butter, divided

1 small onion, finely chopped

4 cups water, divided

3 teaspoons instant chicken bouillon granules

8 ounces assorted wild mushrooms, such as cèpes, shiitake, oyster, portobello, cremini, morels or chanterelles *or* 1 package (8 ounces) sliced mushrooms

1 teaspoon lemon juice

4 tablespoons all-purpose flour

¼ teaspoon white pepper

1 cup half-and-half or whipping cream

Fresh chives (optional)

1. Heat 2 tablespoons butter in medium saucepan over medium-high heat until melted. Add onion; cook and stir until softened. Add 3½ cups water and bouillon; bring to a boil over high heat. Reduce heat to medium-low.

2. Meanwhile, slice stems and caps of shiitake, morel or chanterelle mushrooms; add to broth mixture. Thinly slice stems of cèpes, oyster, portobello or cremini mushrooms; reserve caps. Add to broth mixture; simmer 10 minutes.

3. Slice reserved mushroom caps. Heat 2 tablespoons butter in medium skillet over medium-high heat until melted and bubbly. Add mushrooms; cook and stir until softened. Remove to broth mixture with slotted spoon.

4. Add remaining 2 tablespoons butter and lemon juice to same skillet; heat until butter is melted. Stir in flour and pepper until smooth. Stir in remaining ½ cup water; mix well. Add to broth mixture; cook until soup thickens, stirring constantly. Stir in half-and-half. Garnish with chives.   *Makes 4 servings*

Beef Barley Soup

1 tablespoon vegetable oil

¾ pound boneless beef top round steak, trimmed and cut into ½-inch pieces

3 cans (about 14 ounces each) reduced-sodium beef broth

2 cups unpeeled cubed potatoes

1 can (about 14 ounces) diced tomatoes

1 cup chopped onion

1 cup sliced carrots

½ cup uncooked pearl barley

1 tablespoon cider vinegar

2 teaspoons caraway seeds

2 teaspoons dried marjoram

2 teaspoons dried thyme

½ teaspoon salt

½ teaspoon black pepper

1½ cups sliced green beans (½-inch slices)

1. Heat oil in large saucepan or Dutch oven over medium heat. Add beef; cook and stir until browned on all sides.

2. Stir in broth, potatoes, tomatoes, onion, carrots, barley, vinegar, caraway seeds, marjoram, thyme, salt and pepper; bring to a boil over high heat. Reduce heat to low; cover and simmer 1½ hours. Add green beans; cook, uncovered, 30 minutes or until beef is fork-tender. *Makes 4 servings*

CREAMY IRISH POTATO SOUP

2 tablespoons butter

4 medium green onions, sliced (about ½ cup)

1 stalk celery, sliced (about ½ cup)

**1¾ cups SWANSON® Chicken Broth (Regular, Natural Goodness®
or Certified Organic)**

3 medium potatoes, sliced ¼ inch thick (about 3 cups)

⅛ teaspoon ground black pepper

1½ cups milk

1. Heat the butter in a 3-quart saucepan over medium heat. Add the onions and celery and cook until tender.

2. Stir the broth, potatoes and black pepper in the saucepan and heat to a boil. Reduce the heat to low. Cover and cook for 15 minutes or until the potatoes are tender.

3. Place **half** of the broth mixture and **half** of the milk in a blender or food processor. Cover and blend until smooth. Repeat with the remaining broth mixture and remaining milk. Return to the saucepan and heat through.

Makes 5 servings

COCK-A-LEEKIE SOUP

4 cups reduced-sodium chicken broth

4 cups water

2½ pounds chicken thighs (with bones and skin)

3 stalks celery, sliced

2 bay leaves

5 to 6 large leeks (about 2½ pounds)

½ cup uncooked pearl barley

1 teaspoon salt

1 teaspoon ground allspice

12 pitted prunes, halved

Additional salt and black pepper

1. Combine broth, water, chicken, celery and bay leaves in large saucepan or Dutch oven; bring to a boil over high heat. Reduce heat to low; cover and simmer 30 minutes or until chicken is tender. Remove chicken to cutting board to cool.

2. Meanwhile, trim leeks. Cut off roots, any damaged leaves and very tough tops. Cut in half lengthwise, then cut crosswise into ¾-inch pieces. Wash well in several changes of water.

3. Add leeks, barley, 1 teaspoon salt and allspice to saucepan; cover and simmer 40 minutes or until leeks and barley are tender.

4. Remove skin and bones from chicken; cut into bite-size pieces. Add to soup with prunes; simmer 3 minutes or until prunes soften. Season with additional salt and pepper. *Makes 6 to 8 servings*

SHRIMP BISQUE

¼ cup (½ stick) butter

**1 pound medium raw shrimp, peeled, deveined and coarsely chopped
    into ½-inch pieces**

2 green onions, sliced, plus additional for garnish

1 clove garlic, minced

¼ cup all-purpose flour

1 cup chicken or vegetable broth

3 cups half-and-half

½ teaspoon salt

½ teaspoon grated lemon peel

Dash ground red pepper

2 tablespoons dry white wine (optional)

Whole shrimp (optional)

1. Melt butter in large saucepan over medium heat. Add chopped shrimp, green onions and garlic; cook and stir until shrimp are pink and opaque.

2. Add flour; cook and stir just until bubbly. Stir in broth; bring to a boil. Cook 2 minutes, stirring constantly. Remove from heat.

3. Blend soup in small batches in blender or food processor until smooth. Return soup to saucepan.

4. Stir in half-and-half, salt, lemon peel, red pepper and wine, if desired; cook until heated through. Garnish with whole shrimp, if desired.

Makes 4 servings

HEARTY BEEF SOUP

1 tablespoon vegetable oil

¾ pound round steak, cut into ½-inch cubes

1 large onion, chopped

2 medium carrots, sliced

2 stalks celery, diced

5 cups reduced-sodium beef broth

1 bottle (12 ounces) Irish stout or dark ale

¾ teaspoon dried oregano

½ teaspoon salt

⅛ teaspoon black pepper

1 can (about 15 ounces) kidney beans, rinsed and drained

1 small zucchini, cut into ½-inch pieces

4 ounces mushrooms, sliced

1. Heat oil in large saucepan or Dutch oven over medium heat. Add beef, onion, carrots and celery; cook and stir until beef is no longer pink and vegetables are crisp-tender.

2. Stir in broth, stout, oregano, salt and pepper; bring to a boil over high heat. Reduce heat to medium-low; simmer, uncovered, 45 minutes or until beef is fork-tender.

3. Stir in beans, zucchini and mushrooms; bring to a boil over high heat. Reduce heat to medium-low; simmer, uncovered, 5 minutes or until zucchini is tender.

Makes 6 servings

TWO-CHEESE POTATO AND CAULIFLOWER SOUP

1 tablespoon butter
1 cup chopped onion
2 cloves garlic, minced
5 cups whole milk
1 pound Yukon Gold potatoes, diced
1 pound cauliflower florets
1½ teaspoons salt
⅛ teaspoon ground red pepper
1½ cups (6 ounces) shredded sharp Cheddar cheese
⅓ cup crumbled blue cheese

1. Melt butter in large saucepan or Dutch oven over medium-high heat. Add onion; cook and stir 4 minutes or until translucent. Add garlic; cook and stir 15 seconds.

2. Stir in milk, potatoes, cauliflower, salt and red pepper; bring to a boil. Reduce heat to low; cover and simmer 15 minutes or until potatoes are tender. Cool slightly.

3. Working in batches, blend soup in blender or food processor until smooth. Return to saucepan; cook and stir over medium heat just until heated through. Remove from heat; stir in cheeses until melted.   *Makes 4 to 6 servings*

TIP: One pound of trimmed cauliflower will yield about 1½ cups of florets. You can also substitute 1 pound of frozen cauliflower florets for the fresh florets.

Oyster Chowder

4 slices thick-cut bacon, diced
1¼ cups chopped onion
1 can (about 14 ounces) chicken or vegetable broth
1¼ cups diced peeled potato
1 pint fresh shucked oysters, drained and liquor reserved
1 cup whipping cream or half-and-half
Salt and black pepper
Sliced green onions (optional)

1. Cook bacon in large saucepan over medium heat until crisp, stirring frequently. Drain on paper towel-lined plate.

2. Drain all but about 2 tablespoons drippings from saucepan. Add onion to saucepan; cook and stir 5 minutes or until tender.

3. Add broth, potato and oyster liquor; bring to a boil over high heat. Reduce heat to medium-low; cover and simmer 5 minutes or until potato is tender but firm. Stir in oysters and cream; cook 5 minutes or until edges of oysters begin to curl.

4. Season with salt and pepper; top with bacon and green onions, if desired.

Makes 4 servings

Oxtail Soup

2½ pounds oxtails (beef or veal)
1 large onion, sliced
4 carrots, cut into 1-inch pieces, divided
3 stalks celery, cut into 1-inch pieces, divided
2 sprigs fresh parsley
5 whole black peppercorns
1 bay leaf
4 cups beef broth
1 cup dark beer
2 cups diced baking potatoes
1 teaspoon salt
Chopped fresh parsley (optional)

1. Combine oxtails, onion, half of carrots, one third of celery, parsley sprigs, peppercorns and bay leaf in large saucepan or Dutch oven. Add broth and beer; bring to a boil over high heat. Reduce heat to low; cover and simmer 3 hours or until meat is falling off bones.

2. Remove oxtails to plate; set aside. Strain broth and return to saucepan; skim fat. Add remaining carrots, celery and potatoes to saucepan; bring to a simmer over medium heat. Cook 10 to 15 minutes or until vegetables are tender.

3. Remove meat from oxtails; discard bones. Stir meat and salt into soup; cook until heated through. Sprinkle with chopped parsley, if desired.

Makes 4 servings

DOUBLE PEA SOUP

1 tablespoon vegetable oil
1 onion, finely chopped
3 cloves garlic, minced
4 cups water
2 cups dried split peas
1 bay leaf
1 teaspoon ground mustard
1½ cups frozen green peas
1 teaspoon salt
¼ teaspoon black pepper
Sour cream (optional)

1. Heat oil in large saucepan or Dutch oven over medium-high heat. Add onion; cook 5 minutes or until tender, stirring occasionally. Add garlic; cook and stir 1 minute.

2. Add water, split peas, bay leaf and mustard; bring to a boil over high heat. Reduce heat to medium-low; cover and simmer 45 minutes or until split peas are tender, stirring occasionally.

3. Stir in green peas, salt and pepper; cover and simmer 10 minutes or until green peas are tender. Remove and discard bay leaf. Working in batches, blend soup in blender or food processor until smooth.

4. Top each serving with sour cream, if desired.   *Makes 6 servings*

FISH & SHELLFISH

ROASTED DILL SCROD WITH ASPARAGUS

1 bunch (12 ounces) asparagus spears, trimmed
1 tablespoon olive oil
4 scrod or cod fillets (about 5 ounces each)
1 tablespoon lemon juice
1 teaspoon dried dill weed
½ teaspoon salt
¼ teaspoon black pepper
  Paprika (optional)

1. Preheat oven to 425°F.

2. Place asparagus in 13×9-inch baking dish; drizzle with oil. Roll asparagus to coat lightly with oil; push to edges of dish, stacking asparagus into two layers.

3. Arrange scrod fillets in center of baking dish; drizzle with lemon juice. Combine dill, salt and pepper in small bowl; sprinkle over fish and asparagus.

4. Roast 15 to 17 minutes or until asparagus is crisp-tender and fish is opaque in center and begins to flake when tested with fork. *Makes 4 servings*

Mussels in Beer Broth

2 tablespoons olive oil
⅓ cup chopped shallots
4 cloves garlic, minced
2 cups pale ale or other light-colored beer
1 can (about 14 ounces) seasoned diced tomatoes
¼ cup chopped fresh parsley
1 tablespoon chopped fresh thyme
½ teaspoon salt
¼ teaspoon red pepper flakes
3 pounds mussels, scrubbed and debearded
French bread (optional)

1. Heat oil in large saucepan or Dutch oven over medium heat. Add shallots and garlic; cook and stir 3 minutes or until tender. Stir in beer, tomatoes, parsley, thyme, salt and red pepper flakes; bring to a boil over medium-high heat.

2. Add mussels. Reduce heat to low; cover and simmer 5 to 7 minutes or until mussels open. Discard any unopened mussels. Serve with French bread, if desired.

Makes 4 servings

BAKED COD WITH TOMATOES AND OLIVES

4 cod fillets (about 4 ounces each), cut into 2-inch pieces
    Salt and black pepper
1 can (about 14 ounces) diced tomatoes
2 tablespoons chopped pitted black olives
1 tablespoon olive oil
1 teaspoon minced garlic
2 tablespoons chopped fresh parsley

1. Preheat oven to 400°F. Spray 13×9-inch baking dish with nonstick cooking spray.

2. Arrange cod fillets in prepared baking dish; season with salt and pepper.

3. Combine tomatoes, olives, oil and garlic in medium bowl; mix well. Spoon over fish.

4. Bake 20 minutes or until fish begins to flake when tested with fork. Sprinkle with parsley.   *Makes 4 servings*

SEARED SCALLOPS OVER SPINACH

1 tablespoon olive oil
1 pound sea scallops* (about 12)
¼ teaspoon salt
⅛ teaspoon black pepper
2 cloves garlic, minced
1 shallot, minced
1 package (6 ounces) baby spinach
1 tablespoon lemon juice
   Lemon wedges (optional)

Make sure scallops are dry before adding them to the skillet to ensure that searing will result in a golden crust.

1. Heat oil in large nonstick skillet over medium-high heat. Add scallops; sprinkle with salt and pepper. Cook 2 to 3 minutes per side or until golden. Remove to plate; keep warm.

2. Add garlic and shallot to skillet; cook and stir 45 seconds or until fragrant. Add spinach; cook 2 minutes or just until spinach begins to wilt, stirring occasionally. Remove from heat; stir in lemon juice.

3. Serve scallops over spinach. Garnish with lemon wedges.   *Makes 4 servings*

TROUT WITH MUSHROOMS AND POTATO-PARSNIP MASH

4 medium potatoes, peeled and cut into chunks
4 medium parsnips, peeled and cut into chunks
¼ cup all-purpose flour
½ teaspoon dried thyme
¼ teaspoon salt
¼ teaspoon black pepper
2 fresh whole trout (about 12 ounces each), filleted
4 tablespoons (½ stick) butter, divided
12 ounces cremini mushrooms, sliced
¼ cup dry white or rosé wine
1 tablespoon minced fresh sage

1. Combine potatoes and parsnips in large saucepan; add cold water to cover. Bring to a boil over high heat. Reduce heat to medium-low; simmer until fork-tender.

2. Meanwhile, combine flour, thyme, salt and pepper in shallow dish. Coat trout fillets with flour mixture; shake off excess. Heat 2 tablespoons butter in large skillet over medium-high heat. Add fish to skillet in single layer; cook 1 to 2 minutes per side or until fish begins to flake when tested with fork. Remove to plate; keep warm.

3. Add mushrooms to skillet; cook and stir 3 minutes, adding additional butter if needed to prevent scorching. Season with salt and pepper. Add wine; cook and stir until most of liquid has evaporated.

4. Drain potatoes and parsnips; return to saucepan and mash. Stir in remaining 2 tablespoons butter and sage; season with salt and pepper. Serve trout over mashed vegetables; top with mushrooms. *Makes 4 servings*

BROILED TILAPIA WITH MUSTARD CREAM SAUCE

4 tilapia fillets, about ¾ inch thick (4 ounces each)

¼ teaspoon salt

¼ teaspoon black pepper

½ cup sour cream

2 tablespoons chopped fresh dill

4 teaspoons Dijon mustard

2 teaspoons lemon juice

⅛ teaspoon garlic powder

1. Preheat broiler. Spray rack of broiler pan with nonstick cooking spray.

2. Place tilapia fillets on rack; sprinkle with salt and pepper.

3. Broil 4 to 5 inches from heat 5 to 8 minutes or until fish begins to flake when tested with fork. (It is not necessary to turn fish.)

4. Meanwhile, combine sour cream, dill, mustard, lemon juice and garlic powder in small bowl. Serve over warm fish.   *Makes 4 servings*

PAN-FRIED OYSTERS

¼ cup all-purpose flour

½ teaspoon salt

¼ teaspoon black pepper

2 eggs

½ cup plain dry bread crumbs

5 tablespoons chopped fresh parsley, divided

2 containers (8 ounces each) shucked fresh oysters, rinsed, drained and patted dry *or* 1 pound fresh oysters, shucked and patted dry

Canola oil for frying

5 slices Irish bacon, crisp-cooked and chopped

Lemon wedges

1. Combine flour, salt and pepper in shallow bowl. Beat eggs in another shallow bowl. Combine bread crumbs and 4 tablespoons parsley in third shallow bowl.

2. Working with one oyster at a time, coat with flour mixture, shaking off excess. Dip in eggs, shaking off excess. Roll in bread crumb mixture to coat. Place coated oysters on clean plate.

3. Heat ½ inch of oil in large skillet over medium-high heat until very hot but not smoking (about 370°F). Add one third of oysters; cook about 2 minutes per side or until golden brown. Drain on paper towel-lined plate. Repeat with remaining oysters.

4. Toss oysters with bacon and remaining 1 tablespoon parsley in large bowl. Serve immediately with lemon wedges. *Makes 4 appetizer servings*

POACHED SALMON WITH DILL-LEMON SAUCE

    4 cups water
    1 cup dry white wine
      Peel of 1 lemon
    4 whole black peppercorns
    3 sprigs fresh parsley
    2 sprigs fresh dill, plus additional for garnish
    1 shallot, cut crosswise into thin slices
    4 salmon fillets, about 1 inch thick (6 ounces each)

DILL-LEMON SAUCE
    1 tablespoon lemon juice
    2 teaspoons canola oil
    ¼ cup mayonnaise
    ¼ cup milk
    2 teaspoons chopped fresh dill

1. Combine water, wine, lemon peel, peppercorns, parsley, 2 dill sprigs and shallot in large saucepan; bring to a simmer over medium heat. Simmer gently 15 minutes. (Do not boil.)

2. Reduce heat to just below simmering. Place salmon fillets in liquid; cook 4 to 5 minutes or until fish begins to flake when tested with fork.

3. Meanwhile, combine lemon juice, oil and mayonnaise in small bowl; mix well. Whisk in milk, 1 tablespoon at a time, mixing well after each addition. Stir in chopped dill just before serving.

4. Remove fish from poaching liquid; discard liquid. Top with sauce; garnish with additional dill sprigs. *Makes 4 servings*

Simple Baked Cod

4 cod fillets (about 6 ounces each)
½ teaspoon salt
¼ teaspoon black pepper
¼ cup (½ stick) butter
1 teaspoon chopped fresh thyme
2 teaspoons grated lemon peel
3 tablespoons chopped fresh parsley

1. Position rack in center of oven. Preheat oven to 425°F. Spray large rimmed baking sheet with nonstick cooking spray.

2. Arrange cod fillets on prepared baking sheet; sprinkle with salt and pepper;

3. Bake 12 to 14 minutes or until fish begins to flake when tested with fork.

4. Meanwhile, melt butter in small saucepan over medium heat. Stir in thyme and lemon peel; cook 1 minute. Remove from heat; stir in parsley. Spoon butter mixture over fish. Serve immediately. *Makes 4 servings*

TRADITIONAL MUSSELS IN CREAM

2 tablespoons butter
1 medium onion, chopped
4 cloves garlic, minced
1 sprig fresh thyme
1 bay leaf
¾ cup whipping cream
¼ teaspoon salt
2 pounds mussels, scrubbed and debearded
1 tablespoon lemon juice
   Crusty bread for serving

1. Melt butter in large saucepan over medium-high heat. Add onion and garlic; cook about 2 minutes or until garlic begins to brown slightly. Add thyme and bay leaf; cook 30 seconds. Stir in cream and salt; bring to a boil and cook 1 minute.

2. Add mussels to saucepan; cover and bring to a boil. Cook 4 to 5 minutes or until mussels open. Uncover saucepan; cook 1 minute.

3. Remove from heat; stir in lemon juice. Discard any unopened mussels. Serve immediately in bowls with bread.   *Makes 4 appetizer or 2 main-dish servings*

Seared Scallops with Mushrooms and Leeks

3 tablespoons butter, divided

1½ pounds sea scallops, patted dry

½ teaspoon salt, divided

¼ teaspoon black pepper, divided

1 package (8 ounces) sliced mushrooms

3 medium leeks, white and light green parts only, cut in half crosswise and very thinly sliced lengthwise

2 cloves garlic, minced

½ cup vermouth or dry white wine

⅓ cup whipping cream

¼ cup (1 ounce) shredded Dubliner cheese

1. Melt 1 tablespoon butter in large nonstick skillet over medium-high heat. Sprinkle scallops with ¼ teaspoon salt and ⅛ teaspoon pepper. Add to skillet; cook 2 to 3 minutes per side or until browned and opaque. (Cook in batches if necessary to prevent overcrowding.) Remove scallops to plate; keep warm.

2. Melt remaining 2 tablespoons butter in same skillet over medium-high heat. Add mushrooms; cook 3 to 4 minutes or just until mushrooms begin to brown slightly. Add leeks and garlic; cook and stir 3 to 4 minutes or until leeks are tender. Add vermouth; cook about 2 minutes or until almost evaporated. Stir in cream; bring to a boil and cook 1 minute. Add cheese, remaining ¼ teaspoon salt and ⅛ teaspoon pepper; cook and stir about 30 seconds or until cheese melts.

3. Return scallops to skillet; cook 1 to 2 minutes or until heated through. Serve immediately. *Makes 4 servings*

SOLE WITH LEMON-BUTTER CAPER SAUCE

¼ cup all-purpose flour
½ teaspoon plus ⅛ teaspoon salt, divided
¼ teaspoon black pepper
1 pound Dover sole fillets
2 tablespoons vegetable oil
3 tablespoons butter
2 tablespoons lemon juice
2 teaspoons capers, rinsed, drained and chopped
2 tablespoons finely chopped fresh chives

1. Combine flour, ½ teaspoon salt and pepper in shallow bowl. Coat sole fillets with flour mixture, shaking off excess.

2. Heat oil in large nonstick skillet over medium heat. Add half of fish; cook 2 to 3 minutes per side or until golden brown. Remove to plate; tent with foil to keep warm. Repeat with remaining fish.

3. Wipe out skillet with paper towels. Add butter and remaining ⅛ teaspoon salt; cook 20 to 30 seconds or until melted and lightly browned. Remove from heat; stir in lemon juice and capers.

4. Drizzle sauce over fish; sprinkle with chives. Serve immediately.

Makes 2 servings

LEMON GARLIC SHRIMP

⅓ cup clarified butter*

2 to 4 tablespoons minced garlic

1½ pounds large raw shrimp, peeled and deveined (with tails on)

6 green onions, thinly sliced

¼ cup dry white wine

2 tablespoons lemon juice

Chopped fresh Italian parsley

Salt and black pepper

Lemon wedges (optional)

To clarify butter, melt butter in small saucepan over low heat. Skim off white foam that forms on top, then strain clear butter that remains through cheesecloth. Discard cheesecloth and milky residue in bottom of pan. Store clarified butter in airtight container in refrigerator for up to 2 months.

1. Heat butter in large skillet over medium heat. Add garlic; cook and stir 1 to 2 minutes or until softened but not brown.

2. Add shrimp, green onions, wine and lemon juice; cook 2 to 4 minutes or until shrimp are pink and opaque, stirring occasionally.

3. Sprinkle with parsley; season with salt and pepper. Serve with lemon wedges, if desired.   *Makes 4 to 6 servings*

PAN-ROASTED PIKE WITH BUTTERY BREAD CRUMBS

6 tablespoons butter, divided

2 garlic cloves, minced

⅓ cup plain dry bread crumbs

½ teaspoon salt, divided

4 tablespoons chopped fresh parsley

4 pike fillets or other medium-firm white fish (about 6 ounces each)

⅛ teaspoon black pepper

2 tablespoons lemon juice

1. Preheat oven to 400°F.

2. Melt 2 tablespoons butter in small nonstick skillet over medium-high heat. Add garlic; cook and stir 1 minute or just until lightly browned. Stir in bread crumbs and ⅛ teaspoon salt; cook and stir 1 minute. Transfer to small bowl; stir in parsley.

3. Melt 1 tablespoon butter in large ovenproof skillet over medium-high heat. Sprinkle pike fillets with ¼ teaspoon salt and pepper. Add to skillet, flesh side down; cook 1 minute. Remove from heat; turn fish and top with bread crumb mixture. Transfer to oven; roast 8 to 10 minutes or until fish begins to flake when tested with fork.

4. Wipe out small skillet with paper towel; heat over medium heat. Add remaining 3 tablespoons butter; cook 3 to 4 minutes or until melted and lightly browned, stirring occasionally. Stir in lemon juice and remaining ⅛ teaspoon salt. Spoon mixture over fish just before serving. *Makes 4 servings*

ROASTED SALMON WITH IRISH WHISKEY SAUCE

    4 salmon fillets (about 6 ounces each)
    ½ teaspoon salt, divided
    ⅛ teaspoon black pepper
    ⅓ cup Irish whiskey
    ¼ cup finely chopped shallots
    1 tablespoon white wine vinegar
    ½ cup whipping cream
    1½ teaspoons Dijon mustard
    2 tablespoons butter, cut into small pieces
    2 tablespoons chopped fresh chives

1. Position rack in center of oven. Preheat oven to 425°F. Spray large rimmed baking sheet with nonstick cooking spray.

2. Arrange salmon fillets on prepared baking sheet; sprinkle with ¼ teaspoon salt and pepper.

3. Roast 8 to 10 minutes or until fish begins to flake when tested with fork.

4. Meanwhile, combine whiskey, shallots and vinegar in small saucepan; bring to a boil over medium-high heat. Cook about 4 minutes or until liquid nearly evaporates and mixture looks like wet sand. Stir in cream and mustard; cook and stir 2 minutes or until slightly thickened. Remove from heat; whisk in butter, chives and remaining ¼ teaspoon salt. Spoon sauce over fish. Serve immediately.

Makes 4 servings

MEAT

SAUSAGE AND CABBAGE SKILLET

1 tablespoon plus 1 teaspoon olive oil, divided
1 pound smoked sausage, cut into 2-inch pieces
6 cups coarsely chopped cabbage
1 yellow onion, cut into ½-inch wedges
2 cloves garlic, minced
¾ teaspoon sugar
¼ teaspoon caraway seeds
¼ teaspoon salt
¼ teaspoon black pepper

1. Heat 1 teaspoon oil in large skillet over medium-high heat. Add sausage; cook and stir 3 minutes or until browned. Remove to plate.

2. Heat remaining 1 tablespoon oil in same skillet. Add cabbage, onion, garlic, sugar, caraway seeds, salt and pepper; cook and stir 5 minutes or until onion begins to brown. Add sausage; cover and cook 5 minutes. Remove from heat; let stand 5 minutes. *Makes 4 servings*

IRISH STEW IN BREAD

1½ pounds lean, boned American lamb shoulder, cut into 1-inch cubes
¼ cup all-purpose flour
2 tablespoons vegetable oil
2 cloves garlic, crushed
2 cups water
¼ cup Burgundy wine
5 medium carrots, chopped
3 medium potatoes, peeled and sliced
2 large onions, peeled and chopped
2 ribs celery, sliced
¾ teaspoon black pepper
1 cube beef bouillon, crushed
1 cup frozen peas
¼ pound sliced fresh mushrooms
   Round bread, unsliced*

*Stew can be served individually in small loaves or in one large loaf. Slice bread crosswise near top to form lid. Hollow larger piece, leaving 1-inch border. Fill "bowl" with hot stew; cover with "lid." Serve immediately.

Coat lamb with flour while heating oil in Dutch oven over low heat. Add lamb and garlic; cook and stir until brown. Add water, wine, carrots, potatoes, onions, celery, pepper and bouillon. Cover; simmer 30 to 35 minutes.

Add peas and mushrooms. Cover; simmer 10 minutes. Bring to a boil; adjust seasonings, if necessary. Serve in bread.   *Makes 6 to 8 servings*

Favorite recipe from American Lamb Board

Corned Beef and Cabbage with Horseradish Mustard Sauce

       1 **large onion, cut into chunks**
    1½ **cups baby carrots**
     16 **small (1-inch) red potatoes* (about 1¼ pounds)**
       1 **corned beef brisket (2 to 2½ pounds)**
       ½ **large head cabbage (1 pound), cut into 8 thin wedges**
       ⅓ **cup sour cream**
       ⅓ **cup mayonnaise**
       2 **tablespoons Dijon mustard**
       2 **tablespoons prepared horseradish**

*If 1-inch potatoes are not available, cut larger potatoes into halves or quarters as needed.

Slow Cooker Directions

1. Place onion, carrots and potatoes in slow cooker. Drain corned beef, reserving spice packet and juices from package. Place corned beef on vegetables; pour juices over beef and top with contents of spice packet. Add enough water to barely cover beef and vegetables (about 4 cups). Cover; cook on LOW 8 to 9 hours or on HIGH 5 to 6 hours or until corned beef is fork-tender.

2. Remove corned beef to large sheet of heavy-duty foil; wrap tightly and set aside. Add cabbage to vegetables, pushing down into liquid. Increase heat to HIGH. Cover; cook on HIGH 30 to 40 minutes or until vegetables are tender.

3. Meanwhile, combine sour cream, mayonnaise, mustard and horseradish in small bowl; mix well. Reserve ½ cup of juices in slow cooker. Drain vegetables; transfer to serving platter. Thinly slice corned beef; arrange on platter and drizzle with reserved juices. Serve with horseradish mustard sauce.   *Makes 6 to 8 servings*

STUFFED PORK TENDERLOIN
WITH APPLE RELISH

6 tablespoons (¾ stick) butter
1 onion, chopped
3 cloves garlic
1 cup dry bread crumbs
1 tablespoon chopped fresh parsley
2 teaspoons minced fresh thyme
1 teaspoon minced fresh sage
½ teaspoon salt, divided
¼ teaspoon black pepper
1 egg, lightly beaten
3 to 4 tablespoons dry white wine or apple cider
2 pork tenderloins (about 1 pound each), trimmed
  Apple Relish (recipe follows)

1. Preheat oven to 450°F. Place rack in large roasting pan; spray with nonstick cooking spray.

2. Melt butter in large skillet. Add onion and garlic; cook and stir 2 to 3 minutes or until translucent. Add bread crumbs, parsley, thyme, sage, ¼ teaspoon salt and pepper; mix well. Stir in egg. Add enough wine to moisten stuffing.

3. Cut tenderloins in half horizontally about halfway through and open flat. Cover with plastic wrap; pound to ½-inch thickness. Sprinkle with remaining ¼ teaspoon salt. Spoon half of stuffing down center of each tenderloin. Close meat around stuffing; tie with kitchen string every 3 or 4 inches to secure. Place in prepared pan.

4. Bake 15 minutes. *Reduce heat to 350°F;* bake 45 minutes or until cooked through (145°F). Meanwhile, prepare Apple Relish. Serve with pork.   *Makes 8 servings*

APPLE RELISH: Combine 3 apples, cut into ½-inch pieces, ½ cup chopped green onions, ½ cup golden raisins, ¼ cup chopped crystallized ginger, ¼ cup cider vinegar, 3 tablespoons sugar and 1 tablespoon Irish whiskey in medium saucepan. Cook, partially covered, over medium heat 20 to 30 minutes or until apples are tender but not falling apart. Let cool. Stir in 1 tablespoon chopped fresh mint. Serve warm or cold.

HEARTY SHEPHERD'S PIE

1½ pounds ground beef
2 cups FRENCH'S® French Fried Onions
1 can (10¾ ounces) condensed tomato soup
½ cup water
2 teaspoons Italian seasoning
¼ teaspoon *each* salt and black pepper
1 package (10 ounces) frozen mixed vegetables, thawed
3 cups hot mashed potatoes

1. Preheat oven to 375°F. Cook meat in large ovenproof skillet until browned; drain. Stir in 1 cup French Fried Onions, soup, water, seasoning, salt and pepper.

2. Spoon vegetables over beef mixture. Top with mashed potatoes.

3. Bake 20 minutes or until hot. Sprinkle with remaining French Fried Onions. Bake 2 minutes or until golden. *Makes 6 servings*

Lamb and Potato Hot Pot

　3 tablespoons canola oil, divided
1½ pounds boneless leg of lamb, cut into 1-inch cubes
　4 medium onions, thinly sliced
　3 carrots, thinly sliced
　1 teaspoon chopped fresh thyme
　2 tablespoons all-purpose flour
1¼ cups reduced-sodium chicken broth
　¾ teaspoon salt, divided
　¼ teaspoon black pepper
　3 medium russet potatoes (12 ounces), peeled and thinly sliced
　1 tablespoon butter, cut into small pieces

1. Preheat oven to 350°F. Spray 2-quart casserole with nonstick cooking spray.

2. Heat 2 tablespoons oil in large saucepan over medium-high heat. Add half of lamb; cook 4 to 5 minutes or until browned, turning occasionally. Remove to plate; repeat with remaining lamb.

3. Heat remaining 1 tablespoon oil in same saucepan over medium-high heat. Add onions, carrots and thyme; cook 10 to 12 minutes or until onions are golden, stirring occasionally. Stir in lamb and any accumulated juices; cook 1 minute. Add flour; cook and stir 1 minute. Stir in broth, ½ teaspoon salt and pepper; bring to a boil and cook about 1 minute or until mixture starts to thicken. Transfer to prepared casserole.

4. Arrange potato slices in overlapping layer over lamb mixture, starting from side of casserole and working in towards center. Sprinkle with remaining ¼ teaspoon salt; dot with butter. Cover tightly with foil.

5. Bake 1 hour. Uncover; bake 15 to 20 minutes or until potatoes just begin to brown at edges and lamb is tender. *Makes 4 to 6 servings*

Sage-Roasted Pork with Rutabaga

   1 bunch fresh sage

   4 cloves garlic, minced (2 tablespoons)

1½ teaspoons coarse salt, divided

   1 teaspoon coarsely ground pepper, divided

   5 tablespoons extra virgin olive oil, divided

   1 boneless pork loin roast (2 to 2½ pounds)

   2 medium or 1 large rutabaga (1 to 1½ pounds), peeled and cut
      into 1½-inch pieces

   4 carrots, cut into 1½-inch pieces

1. Chop enough sage to measure 2 tablespoons; reserve remaining sage. Mash chopped sage, garlic, ½ teaspoon salt and ½ teaspoon pepper in small bowl to form paste. Stir in 2 tablepoons oil.

2. Score fatty side of pork roast with sharp knife, making cuts about ¼ inch deep. Rub herb paste into cuts and onto all sides of pork. Place pork on large plate; cover and refrigerate 1 to 2 hours.

3. Preheat oven to 400°F. Spray large casserole or roasting pan with nonstick cooking spray. Place rutabaga and carrots in large bowl. Drizzle with remaining 3 tablespoons oil and sprinkle with remaining 1 teaspoon salt and ½ teaspoon pepper; toss to coat.

4. Arrange vegetables in single layer in prepared pan. Place pork on top of vegetables, scraping any remaining herb paste from plate into roasting pan. Tuck 3 sprigs of remaining sage into vegetables.

5. Roast 15 minutes. *Reduce oven temperature to 325°F.* Roast 45 minutes to 1 hour 15 minutes or until pork is 145°F and barely pink in center, stirring vegetables once or twice during cooking time. Let pork stand 5 minutes before slicing. *Makes 4 to 6 servings*

STEAK AND MUSHROOM PIE

3 tablespoons butter

1½ pounds beef chuck steak, cut into 1-inch cubes

2 medium onions, chopped

3 stalks celery, cut into ½-inch slices

1 package (8 ounces) sliced mushrooms

½ teaspoon dried thyme

½ cup red wine

¼ cup all-purpose flour

1 cup reduced-sodium beef broth

2 tablespoons tomato paste

1 tablespoon Dijon mustard

½ teaspoon salt

¼ teaspoon black pepper

1 refrigerated pie crust (half of 15-ounce package)

1 egg, lightly beaten

1. Spray deep-dish pie plate or 1½-quart baking dish with nonstick cooking spray. Melt 2 tablespoons butter in large saucepan over medium-high heat. Add half of beef; cook 4 to 5 minutes or until browned, turning occasionally. Remove to plate; repeat with remaining beef.

2. Melt remaining 1 tablespoon butter in same saucepan over medium-high heat. Add onions, celery, mushrooms and thyme; cook and stir 4 to 5 minutes or until vegetables begin to soften. Add wine; cook and stir 3 to 4 minutes or until almost evaporated. Add flour; cook and stir 1 minute. Stir in broth, tomato paste and mustard; bring to a boil. Reduce heat to medium-low; cover and simmer about 65 minutes or until beef is tender, stirring occasionally. Remove from heat; stir in salt and pepper. Transfer mixture to prepared pie plate; let cool 20 minutes.

3. Preheat oven to 400°F. Roll out pie crust on lightly floured surface to fit top of pie plate. Place crust over filling; decoratively flute or crimp edges. Brush crust with egg; cut several small slits in top of crust with tip of knife.

4. Bake 23 to 25 minutes or until crust is golden. Cool 5 minutes before serving.

Makes 4 to 6 servings

MINT MARINATED RACKS OF LAMB

2 whole racks (6 ribs each) lamb rib chops (about 3 pounds), well trimmed
1 cup dry red wine
½ cup plus 2 tablespoons chopped fresh mint, divided
3 cloves garlic, minced
¼ cup Dijon mustard
⅔ cup plain dry bread crumbs

1. Place lamb in large resealable food storage bag. Combine wine, ½ cup mint and garlic in small bowl. Pour over lamb chops. Seal bag; turn to coat. Marinate in refrigerator at least 2 hours or up to 4 hours, turning occasionally.

2. Prepare grill for indirect cooking.

3. Remove lamb from marinade; discard marinade. Pat lamb dry with paper towels; place in shallow dish. Combine mustard and remaining 2 tablespoons mint in small bowl; spread over meaty side of lamb. Pat bread crumbs evenly over mustard mixture.

4. Place lamb, crumb side down, on grid. Grill, covered, over medium heat 10 minutes. Turn lamb and grill, covered, 20 minutes for medium or to desired doneness. Remove lamb to cutting board; let stand 5 minutes before slicing. Cut lamb between ribs into individual chops. *Makes 4 servings*

Spiced Honey Glazed Ham

1 smoked bone-in spiral-cut ham (8 pounds)
½ cup clover honey or other mild honey
2 tablespoons spicy brown mustard
2 tablespoons apple cider vinegar
1 teaspoon finely grated orange peel
¼ teaspoon black pepper
⅛ teaspoon ground cloves

1. Position rack in lower third of oven. Preheat oven to 325°F.

2. Line large rimmed baking sheet with heavy-duty foil; place wire rack over foil. Place ham on rack; cover loosely with foil. Pour 2 cups water into pan. Bake 1½ hours.

3. Meanwhile, combine honey, mustard, vinegar, orange peel, pepper and cloves in small saucepan; bring to a boil over medium-high heat. Remove from heat; set aside to cool.

4. Remove ham from oven. *Increase oven temperature to 400°F.* Brush ham with glaze; bake, uncovered, 40 minutes or until shiny golden brown crust has formed, brushing with glaze every 10 minutes.

5. Remove ham to cutting board. Let stand 10 minutes before slicing.

Makes 12 to 14 servings

Sirloin with Mushrooms and Whiskey-Cream Sauce

2 tablespoons butter

1 tablespoon vegetable oil

8 ounces cremini mushrooms, sliced

1½ pounds sirloin steak

½ teaspoon salt

¼ teaspoon black pepper

½ cup Irish whiskey

½ cup whipping cream

½ cup reduced-sodium beef broth

Chopped fresh chives

1. Heat butter and oil in large skillet over medium-high heat. Add mushrooms; cook and stir 8 minutes or until liquid evaporates. Transfer to bowl.

2. Sprinkle both sides of steak with salt and pepper. Add to skillet; cook about 3 minutes per side or to desired doneness. Remove to plate; keep warm.

3. Add whiskey to skillet; cook and stir 2 minutes, scraping up browned bits from bottom of skillet. Add cream and broth; cook and stir 3 minutes. Stir in any accumulated juices from steak.

4. Return mushrooms to skillet; cook and stir 2 minutes or until sauce thickens. Pour sauce over steak; sprinkle with chives.   *Makes 4 servings*

ROASTED DIJON LAMB WITH HERBS AND COUNTRY VEGETABLES

20 **cloves garlic, peeled (about 2 medium heads)**
¼ **cup Dijon mustard**
2 **tablespoons water**
2 **tablespoons fresh rosemary leaves**
1 **tablespoon fresh thyme**
1¼ **teaspoons salt, divided**
1 **teaspoon black pepper**
4½ **pounds boneless leg of lamb,* trimmed**
1 **pound parsnips, cut diagonally into ½-inch pieces**
1 **pound carrots, cut diagonally into ½-inch pieces**
2 **large onions, cut into ½-inch wedges**
3 **tablespoons extra virgin olive oil, divided**

*If unavailable, substitute packaged marinated lamb and rinse it off.

1. Combine garlic, mustard, water, rosemary, thyme, ¾ teaspoon salt and pepper in food processor; process until smooth. Place lamb in large bowl or baking pan. Spoon garlic mixture over top and sides of lamb; cover and refrigerate at least 8 hours.

2. Preheat oven to 500°F. Line broiler pan with foil; top with broiler rack. Spray rack with nonstick cooking spray. Combine parsnips, carrots, onions and 2 tablespoons oil in large bowl; toss to coat. Spread on broiler rack; top with lamb.

3. Roast 15 minutes. *Reduce oven temperature to 325°F.* Roast 1 hour and 20 minutes or until 155°F for medium or until desired doneness.

4. Remove lamb to cutting board; let stand 10 minutes before slicing. Continue roasting vegetables 10 minutes.

5. Transfer vegetables to large bowl. Add remaining 1 tablespoon oil and ½ teaspoon salt; toss to coat. Thinly slice lamb; serve with vegetables.   *Makes 12 servings*

CIDER PORK AND ONIONS

2 to 3 tablespoons vegetable oil

4 to 4½ pounds bone-in pork shoulder roast (pork butt)

4 to 5 medium onions, sliced (about 4 cups)

1 teaspoon salt, divided

4 cloves garlic, minced

3 sprigs fresh rosemary

½ teaspoon black pepper

2 to 3 cups apple cider

1. Preheat oven to 325°F. Heat 2 tablespoons oil in Dutch oven over medium-high heat. Add pork; cook until browned on all sides. Remove to plate.

2. Add onions and ½ teaspoon salt to Dutch oven; cook and stir 10 minutes or until translucent, adding additional oil as needed to prevent scorching. Add garlic; cook and stir 1 minute. Add pork and rosemary; sprinkle with remaining ½ teaspoon salt and pepper. Add cider to come about halfway up sides of pork.

3. Cover and bake 2 to 2½ hours or until very tender. (Meat should be almost falling off bones.) Remove to large platter; keep warm.

4. Remove rosemary sprigs from Dutch oven. Boil liquid in Dutch oven over medium-high heat about 20 minutes or until reduced by half; skim fat. Season with additional salt and pepper, if desired. Slice pork; serve with sauce.

Makes 8 servings

Beef Stew

2 tablespoons olive or vegetable oil

3 pounds beef chuck, trimmed and cut into 2-inch pieces

2 teaspoons salt

½ teaspoon black pepper

3 medium sweet or yellow onions, halved and sliced

6 medium carrots, cut into ½-inch pieces

8 ounces sliced mushrooms

4 ounces smoked ham, cut into ¼-inch pieces

2 tablespoons minced garlic

1 bottle (about 12 ounces) Irish stout

1 can (about 14 ounces) reduced-sodium beef broth

1 teaspoon sugar

1 teaspoon dried thyme

1 teaspoon Worcestershire sauce

⅓ cup cold water

2 tablespoons cornstarch

3 tablespoons chopped fresh parsley

Hot cooked noodles or steamed red potatoes (optional)

1. Heat oil in Dutch oven over medium-high heat. Add half of beef; sprinkle with salt and pepper. Cook about 8 minutes or until browned on all sides. Remove to bowl; repeat with remaining beef.

2. Add onions; cook and stir over medium heat about 10 minutes. Stir in carrots, mushrooms, ham and garlic; cook and stir 10 minutes or until vegetables are softened, scraping up any browned bits from bottom of Dutch oven.

3. Return beef to Dutch oven; add stout and broth. (Liquid should just cover beef and vegetables; add water if needed.) Stir in sugar, thyme and Worcestershire

sauce; bring to a boil. Reduce heat to low; cover and simmer 2 hours or until beef is fork-tender.

4. Skim fat. Stir ⅓ cup water into cornstarch in small bowl until smooth. Whisk into stew; simmer 5 minutes. Stir in parsley. Serve over noodles, if desired.

Makes 8 servings

LAMB CHOPS WITH MUSTARD SAUCE

1 teaspoon dried thyme
½ teaspoon salt
¼ teaspoon black pepper
4 lamb loin chops (about 6 ounces each)
2 tablespoons canola or vegetable oil
¼ cup finely chopped shallots or sweet onion
¼ cup beef or chicken broth
2 tablespoons Worcestershire sauce
1½ tablespoons Dijon mustard
   Fresh thyme sprigs (optional)

1. Sprinkle dried thyme, salt and pepper over lamb chops. Heat oil in large skillet over medium heat. Add lamb; cook 4 minutes per side. Remove to plate.

2. Add shallots to same skillet; cook 3 minutes, stirring occasionally. Add broth, Worcestershire sauce and mustard; simmer 5 minutes over medium-low heat or until sauce thickens slightly, stirring occasionally.

3. Return lamb to skillet; cook 2 minutes for medium-rare, turning once. Garnish with fresh thyme. *Makes 4 servings*

POULTRY

Irish Stout Chicken

2 tablespoons vegetable oil
1 medium onion, chopped
2 cloves garlic, minced
1 whole chicken (3 to 4 pounds), cut into serving pieces
5 carrots, chopped
2 parsnips, peeled and chopped
1 teaspoon dried thyme
¾ teaspoon salt
½ teaspoon black pepper
¾ cup Irish stout
8 ounces sliced mushrooms
¾ cup frozen peas

1. Heat oil in large skillet over medium heat. Add onion and garlic; cook and stir 3 minutes or until tender. Transfer to small bowl.

2. Add chicken to same skillet in single layer; cook over medium-high heat 5 minutes per side or until lightly browned.

3. Add onion mixture, carrots, parsnips, thyme, salt and pepper to skillet. Add stout; bring to a boil over high heat. Reduce heat to low; cover and simmer 35 minutes.

4. Add mushrooms and peas to skillet; cover and cook 10 minutes. Uncover and cook over medium heat 10 minutes or until sauce is slightly thickened and chicken is cooked through (165°F). *Makes 4 servings*

Roast Duck With Apple Stuffing

1 duck (about 5 pounds)
Coarse salt and black pepper
2 tablespoons butter
1 small onion, chopped
2 stalks celery, chopped
3 apples, peeled and cut into bite-size pieces
½ cup chopped mixed dried fruit (prunes, apricots, etc.)
5 to 6 fresh sage leaves (tear large leaves in half)
1 cup dried bread cubes (¼- to ½-inch pieces)
Juice of 1 lemon
1 cup plus 1 tablespoon chicken broth, divided
⅔ cup dry white wine

1. Discard neck, giblets and liver from duck (or reserve for another use); trim fat. Rinse duck thoroughly; pat dry with paper towels. Generously season outside of duck and cavity with salt and pepper. Place duck on rack in roasting pan. Refrigerate, uncovered, 1 to 3 hours until ready to cook.

2. For stuffing, melt butter in medium skillet over medium-high heat. Add onion and celery; cook and stir 2 minutes. Add apples, dried fruit and sage; cook and stir 10 minutes or until apples and vegetables are softened. Combine apple mixture and bread cubes in medium bowl; season with ½ teaspoon salt and ¼ teaspoon pepper. Stir in lemon juice. If stuffing seems dry, add 1 tablespoon broth.

3. Preheat oven to 350°F. Spoon stuffing into duck cavity, packing tightly. Tie legs together with kitchen string. Cut through duck skin in crisscross pattern over breast and legs, being careful to only cut though skin and fat layer (about ¼ inch thick), but not into duck flesh. (Cuts will help render duck fat and make skin crisp.)

4. Roast 1½ to 2 hours or until juices run clear and thermometer inserted into leg joint registers 175°F, rotating pan every 20 minutes. (Temperature of stuffing should reach 165°F.) Remove duck to cutting board. Pour off fat from pan; refrigerate or freeze for another use or discard.

5. For sauce, place roasting pan over medium-high heat. Add wine; cook and stir 5 minutes or until wine is reduced by half, scraping up browned bits from bottom of pan. Add remaining 1 cup broth; cook and stir 2 minutes. Strain sauce; serve with duck and stuffing. *Makes 4 servings*

CHICKEN WITH SWISS CHARD

2 slices bacon, chopped

1 cup chopped onion

1 pound Swiss chard, trimmed and coarsely chopped (6 cups packed)

1 egg white

1 teaspoon water

¼ cup unseasoned dry bread crumbs

2 teaspoons olive oil

1 pound chicken cutlets*

Lemon wedges (optional)

Chicken cutlets are fresh boneless skinless chicken breast halves that have been sliced about ⅓ inch thick. If they aren't available, pound four 4-ounce chicken breast halves to ⅓-inch thickness.

1. Cook bacon and onion in large saucepan over medium heat 6 to 8 minutes or until onion is golden brown. Add chard; cover and cook 2 minutes to wilt. Stir mixture; cook, uncovered, 10 minutes or until chard is tender, stirring occasionally.

2. Meanwhile, beat egg white and water in shallow bowl. Place bread crumbs in another shallow bowl. Dip each chicken cutlet in egg white, shaking off excess. Roll in bread crumbs to coat.

3. Heat oil in large nonstick skillet over medium-high heat. Add chicken cutlets; cook 3 minutes or until golden brown on bottom. Turn cutlets; cook over medium heat 3 to 4 minutes or until golden brown and no longer pink in center. (Watch carefully to avoid burning.) Serve over chard mixture; garnish with lemon wedges. *Makes 4 servings*

ROSEMARY CHICKEN AND ROASTED VEGETABLES

1 (3-pound) whole broiler-fryer chicken
1 tablespoon butter, melted
4 medium red potatoes, cut into quarters
2 cups fresh or frozen whole baby carrots
2 stalks celery, cut into 2-inch pieces (about 1½ cups)
12 small white onions, peeled
1½ teaspoons chopped fresh rosemary leaves or ½ teaspoon dried
    rosemary leaves, crushed
1 cup SWANSON® Chicken Stock
½ cup orange juice

1. Brush the chicken with the butter. Place the chicken and vegetables into a 17×11-inch roasting pan. Season with the rosemary. Stir the stock and orange juice in a small bowl and pour **half** the stock mixture over the chicken and vegetables.

2. Roast at 375°F. for 45 minutes.

3. Stir the vegetables. Add the remaining stock mixture to the pan. Roast for 30 minutes or until the chicken is cooked through.   *Makes 4 servings*

KITCHEN TIP: To quickly peel the onions, place them into a medium bowl. Pour boiling water over the onions to cover. Let stand for 5 minutes. Drain and slip off the skins.

Chicken and Herb Stew

½ cup all-purpose flour

½ teaspoon salt

¼ teaspoon black pepper

¼ teaspoon paprika

4 chicken drumsticks

4 chicken thighs

2 tablespoons olive oil

12 ounces new potatoes, quartered

2 carrots, quartered lengthwise and cut into 3-inch pieces

1 green bell pepper, cut into thin strips

¾ cup chopped onion

2 cloves garlic, minced

1¾ cups water

¼ cup dry white wine

2 cubes chicken bouillon

1 tablespoon chopped fresh oregano

1 teaspoon chopped fresh rosemary

2 tablespoons chopped fresh Italian parsley (optional)

1. Combine flour, salt, black pepper and paprika in shallow dish. Coat chicken with flour mixture, shaking off excess.

2. Heat oil in large skillet over medium-high heat. Add chicken; cook 10 minutes or until browned on both sides, turning once. Remove to plate.

3. Add potatoes, carrots, bell pepper, onion and garlic to same skillet; cook and stir 5 minutes or until lightly browned. Add water, wine and bouillon; cook 1 minute, stirring to scrape up browned bits from bottom of skillet. Stir in oregano and rosemary.

4. Place chicken on top of vegetable mixture, turning several times to coat. Cover and simmer 45 to 50 minutes or until chicken is cooked through (165°F), turning occasionally. Garnish with parsley.   *Makes 4 servings*

Pan-Roasted Chicken Breasts

4 boneless skin-on chicken breasts (about 6 ounces each)
  Salt and black pepper
2 tablespoons vegetable oil
1 medium shallot, finely chopped (about ¼ cup)
1 tablespoon all-purpose flour
½ cup India Pale Ale
½ cup reduced-sodium chicken broth
¼ cup whipping cream
 1 teaspoon Dijon mustard
½ teaspoon finely chopped thyme
¼ teaspoon salt
⅛ teaspoon black pepper
½ cup (2 ounces) shredded Gruyère or Emmental cheese

1. Preheat oven to 375°F.

2. Season both sides of chicken breasts with salt and black pepper. Heat oil in large ovenproof skillet over medium-high heat until almost smoking. Add chicken, skin side down; cook 8 to 10 minutes or until until skin is golden browned. Turn chicken; transfer skillet to oven. Roast about 15 minutes or until no longer pink in center. Remove chicken to plate; tent with foil to keep warm.

3. Add shallot to same skillet; cook and stir over medium heat until softened. Add flour; cook and stir 1 minute. Add ale; cook until reduced by half, stirring to scrape up browned bits from bottom of skillet . Stir in broth, cream, mustard, thyme, ¼ teaspoon salt and ⅛ teaspoon black pepper; cook until slightly thickened.

4. Remove from heat; whisk in cheese until melted and smooth. Spoon sauce over chicken. Serve immediately. *Makes 4 servings*

GLAZED CORNISH HENS

2 fresh or thawed frozen Cornish hens (1½ pounds each)

3 tablespoons lemon juice

1 clove garlic, minced

¼ cup orange marmalade

1 tablespoon coarse grain or country-style mustard

2 teaspoons grated fresh ginger

1. Remove giblets from cavities of hens; reserve for another use or discard. Split hens in half with sharp knife or poultry shears, cutting through breastbones and backbones. Rinse with cold water; pat dry with paper towels. Place hens in large resealable food storage bag.

2. Combine lemon juice and garlic in small bowl; pour over hens. Seal bag; turn to coat. Marinate in refrigerator 30 minutes.

3. Prepare grill for direct cooking.

4. Remove hens from marinade; discard marinade. Place hens, skin side up, on grid. Grill hens, covered, over medium-high heat 20 minutes.

5. Meanwhile, combine marmalade, mustard and ginger in small bowl; mix well. Brush half of marmalade mixture over hens. Grill, covered, 10 minutes. Brush with remaining mixture; grill, covered, 5 to 10 minutes or until cooked through (165°F). Serve immediately. *Makes 4 servings*

Roasted Chicken Thighs with Mustard-Cream Sauce

8 bone-in skin-on chicken thighs
¾ teaspoon black pepper, divided
¼ teaspoon plus ⅛ teaspoon salt, divided
2 teaspoons vegetable oil
2 shallots, thinly sliced
½ Granny Smith apple, peeled and cut into ¼-inch pieces
½ cup chicken broth
½ cup whipping cream
1 tablespoon spicy brown mustard
½ teaspoon chopped fresh thyme

1. Preheat oven to 400°F.

2. Sprinkle both sides of chicken with ½ teaspoon pepper and ¼ teaspoon salt. Heat oil in large ovenproof skillet over medium-high heat. Add chicken, skin side down; cook 8 to 10 minutes or until skin is golden brown. Remove chicken to plate; drain excess fat from skillet.

3. Return chicken to skillet, skin side up. Transfer skillet to oven; roast about 25 minutes or until cooked through (165°F). Remove chicken to clean plate; tent with foil to keep warm.

4. Drain all but 1 tablespoon fat from skillet; heat over medium heat. Add shallots and apple; cook and stir about 8 minutes or until tender. Stir in broth; cook over medium-high heat 1 minute or until reduced by half, scraping up browned bits from bottom of skillet. Add cream, mustard, thyme, remaining ¼ teaspoon pepper and ⅛ teaspoon salt; cook and stir about 2 minutes or until slightly thickened. Spoon sauce over chicken.   *Makes 4 servings*

CRISPY MUSTARD CHICKEN

4 bone-in chicken breasts
   Salt and black pepper
⅓ cup Dijon mustard
½ cup panko bread crumbs or coarse dry bread crumbs

1. Preheat oven to 350°F. Spray rack of broiler pan or shallow baking pan with nonstick cooking spray.

2. Remove skin from chicken. Season chicken with salt and pepper; place on prepared rack. Bake 20 minutes.

3. Brush chicken generously with mustard. Sprinkle with panko and gently press panko into mustard. Bake 20 to 25 minutes or until chicken is cooked through (165°F).   *Makes 4 servings*

HERB ROASTED CHICKEN

1 whole chicken (3 to 4 pounds)
1¼ teaspoons salt, divided
½ teaspoon black pepper, divided
1 lemon, cut into quarters
4 sprigs fresh rosemary, divided
4 sprigs fresh thyme, divided
4 cloves garlic, peeled
2 tablespoons olive oil

1. Preheat oven to 425°F. Place chicken, breast side up, in shallow roasting pan. Season cavity of chicken with ½ teaspoon salt and ¼ teaspoon pepper. Fill cavity with lemon quarters, 2 sprigs rosemary, 2 sprigs thyme and garlic cloves.

2. Chop remaining rosemary and thyme leaves; combine with oil, remaining ¾ teaspoon salt and ¼ teaspoon pepper in small bowl. Brush mixture over chicken.

3. Roast 30 minutes. *Reduce oven temperature to 375°F;* roast 35 to 45 minutes or until cooked through (165°F). Let stand 10 to 15 minutes before carving.

Makes 4 servings

SIDE DISHES

CABBAGE COLCANNON

1 pound new red potatoes, halved
1 tablespoon vegetable oil
1 onion, thinly sliced
½ small head green cabbage, thinly sliced
   Salt and black pepper
3 tablespoons butter

1. Place potatoes in medium saucepan; add cold water to cover by 2 inches. Bring to a boil over medium heat; cook about 20 minutes or until tender. Drain potatoes.

2. Meanwhile, heat oil in large nonstick skillet over medium-high heat. Add onion; cook and stir 8 minutes or until onion is lightly browned. Add cabbage; cook and stir 5 minutes or until softened.

3. Add potatoes to skillet; cook until heated through. Slightly mash potatoes. Season to taste with salt and pepper. Top with butter just before serving.

Makes 6 servings

Potato Cakes with Brussels Sprouts

2½ pounds Yukon Gold potatoes, peeled and cut into 1-inch cubes
6 tablespoons butter, melted
⅓ cup milk, warmed
2 teaspoons salt
½ teaspoon black pepper
3 tablespoons vegetable oil, divided
12 ounces brussels sprouts, ends trimmed, thinly sliced
4 green onions, thinly sliced on the diagonal

1. Place potatoes in large saucepan or Dutch oven; add cold water to cover by 2 inches. Bring to a boil over high heat. Reduce heat to medium-low; cover and simmer about 10 minutes or until tender. Drain potatoes.

2. Return potatoes to saucepan; mash with potato masher until slightly chunky. Stir in butter, milk, salt and pepper until well blended; set aside.

3. Heat 1 tablespoon oil in large nonstick skillet over medium-high heat. Add brussels sprouts; cook about 8 minutes or until tender and lightly browned, stirring occasionally. Stir brussels sprouts and green onions into potato mixture. Wipe out skillet with paper towel.

4. Heat 1 tablespoon oil in skillet over medium heat. Drop potato mixture into skillet by ½ cupfuls, spacing about ½ inch apart. (Use spoon to remove mixture from cup if necessary.) Cook about 3 minutes per side or until cakes are browned and crisp, pressing down lightly with spatula. Remove to platter; tent with foil to keep warm. Repeat with remaining 1 tablespoon oil and potato mixture.

Makes 12 cakes

YORKSHIRE PUDDING

1 cup milk

2 eggs

½ teaspoon salt

1 cup all-purpose flour

¼ cup reserved drippings from roast or melted butter

1. Combine milk, eggs and salt in blender or food processor; blend 15 seconds. Add flour; blend 2 minutes. Let batter stand in blender at room temperature 30 minutes to 1 hour.

2. Preheat oven to 450°F. Place meat drippings in 9-inch square baking pan. Heat in oven 5 minutes.

3. Blend batter 10 seconds; pour into hot drippings. *Do not stir.* Immediately return pan to oven. Bake 20 minutes. *Reduce oven temperature to 350°F;* bake 10 minutes or until pudding is golden brown and puffed. Cut into squares. Serve warm. *Makes 6 to 8 servings*

Beet and Arugula Salad

3 medium beets, trimmed
6 cups baby arugula
2 tablespoons chopped shallots
1 tablespoon white wine vinegar
1 teaspoon Dijon mustard
¼ teaspoon salt
⅛ teaspoon black pepper
3 tablespoons extra virgin olive oil
4 wedges (1 ounce each) aged Irish Cheddar cheese

1. Place beets in medium saucepan; add cold water to cover by 2 inches. Bring to a boil over medium-high heat; cook 35 to 40 minutes or until beets can be easily pierced with tip of knife. Drain beets; cool 15 minutes.

2. Peel beets; cut into ½-inch cubes. Place in medium bowl. Place arugula in separate medium bowl. Combine shallots, vinegar, mustard, salt and pepper in small bowl. Slowly whisk in oil until well blended. Toss beets with 1 tablespoon dressing. Toss arugula with remaining dressing.

3. Divide arugula among four plates. Top with beets; garnish with wedge of cheese. Serve immediately.   *Makes 4 servings*

ROASTED CAULIFLOWER WITH CHEDDAR BEER SAUCE

1 large head cauliflower (about 2½ pounds), trimmed and cut into
   ½-inch florets
2 tablespoons vegetable oil, divided
½ teaspoon salt, divided
½ teaspoon black pepper
2 medium shallots, finely chopped
2 teaspoons all-purpose flour
½ cup Irish ale
1 tablespoon spicy brown mustard
1 tablespoon Worcestershire sauce
1½ cups (6 ounces) shredded Cheddar cheese

1. Preheat oven to 450°F. Line large baking sheet with foil.

2. Combine cauliflower, 1 tablespoon oil, ¼ teaspoon salt and pepper in medium bowl; toss to coat. Spread in single layer on prepared baking sheet. Roast about 25 minutes or until tender and lightly browned, stirring occasionally.

3. Meanwhile, heat remaining 1 tablespoon oil in medium saucepan over medium heat. Add shallots; cook and stir 3 to 4 minutes or until tender. Add flour and remaining ¼ teaspoon salt; cook and stir 1 minute. Add ale, mustard and Worcestershire sauce; bring to a simmer over medium-high heat. Reduce heat to medium-low; add cheese by ¼ cupfuls, stirring until cheese is melted before adding next addition. Cover and keep warm over low heat, stirring occasionally.

4. Place roasted cauliflower in serving bowl; top with cheese sauce. Serve immediately.   *Makes 4 to 6 servings (1¼ cups sauce)*

Boxty Pancakes

2 medium russet potatoes (1 pound), peeled, divided
⅔ cup all-purpose flour
1 teaspoon baking powder
½ teaspoon salt
⅔ cup low-fat buttermilk
3 tablespoons butter

1. Cut one potato into 1-inch chunks; place in small saucepan and add cold water to cover by 2 inches. Bring to a boil over medium-high heat; cook 14 to 18 minutes or until tender. Drain potato; return to saucepan and mash. Transfer to medium bowl.

2. Shred remaining potato on large holes of box grater; add to bowl with mashed potato. Stir in flour, baking powder and salt until blended. Stir in buttermilk.

3. Melt 1 tablespoon butter in large nonstick skillet over medium heat. Drop four slightly heaping tablespoonfuls of batter into skillet; flatten into 2½-inch circles. Cook about 4 minutes per side or until golden and puffed. Remove to plate; cover to keep warm. Repeat with remaining batter and butter. Serve immediately.

Makes 4 servings (16 to 20 pancakes)

SERVING SUGGESTION: Serve with melted butter, sour cream or maple syrup.

BRAISED LEEKS

3 to 4 large leeks (1½ to 2 pounds)
¼ cup (½ stick) butter
¼ teaspoon salt
¼ teaspoon pepper
¼ cup dry white wine
¼ cup reduced-sodium chicken or vegetable broth
3 to 4 sprigs fresh parsley

1. Trim green stem ends of leeks; remove any damaged outer leaves. Slice leeks lengthwise up to, but not through, root ends to hold leeks together. Rinse leeks in cold water, separating layers to remove embedded dirt. Cut leeks crosswise into 3-inch lengths; cut off and discard root ends.

2. Melt butter in skillet large enough to hold leeks in single layer. Arrange leeks in skillet in crowded layer, keeping pieces together as much as possible. Cook over medium-high heat about 8 minutes or until leeks begin to color and soften, turning with tongs once or twice. Sprinkle with salt and pepper.

3. Add wine, broth and parsley; bring to a simmer. Cover and cook over low heat 20 minutes or until leeks are very tender. Remove parsley sprigs before serving.

Makes 4 servings

TIP: Leeks often contain a lot of embedded dirt between their layers, so they need to be washed thoroughly. It's easiest to slice up to—but not through—the root ends before slicing or chopping so the leeks hold together while washing them.

SERVING SUGGESTION: Top the braised leeks with toasted bread crumbs, cheese or crisp crumbled bacon for an extra-rich side dish.

MASHED CARROTS AND PARSNIPS

1 medium russet potato, peeled and cut into 1-inch pieces
3 parsnips, peeled and cut into 1-inch pieces
3 carrots, cut into 1-inch pieces
1 tablespoon honey
¼ cup (½ stick) butter, softened
½ teaspoon salt
¼ teaspoon black pepper

1. Place potato in large saucepan; add cold water to cover by 2 inches. Bring to a boil over medium-high heat; cook about 7 minutes or until potato is partially cooked.

2. Add parsnips, carrots, and honey to saucepan; return to a boil. Cook 16 to 18 minutes or until vegetables are tender. Drain vegetables; return to saucepan.

3. Add butter, salt and pepper to vegetables; mash until smooth. Serve hot.

Makes 4 to 6 servings

Kale with Lemon and Garlic

2 bunches kale or Swiss chard (1 to 1¼ pounds)
1 tablespoon olive or vegetable oil
3 cloves garlic, minced
½ cup reduced-sodium chicken or vegetable broth
½ teaspoon salt
¼ teaspoon black pepper
1 lemon, cut into 8 wedges

1. Trim tough stems from kale. Stack and thinly slice leaves.

2. Heat oil in large saucepan over medium heat. Add garlic; cook and stir 3 minutes. Add kale and broth; cover and simmer 7 minutes. Stir kale; cover and simmer over medium-low heat 8 to 10 minutes or until kale is tender.

3. Season with salt and pepper. Squeeze wedge of lemon over each serving.

Makes 8 servings

Stovies with Bacon

3 medium russet potatoes (about 1½ pounds), peeled
6 slices bacon
2 large onions, halved vertically and sliced
4 teaspoons butter
½ teaspoon salt
⅛ teaspoon black pepper
⅓ cup water

1. Place potatoes in large saucepan; add cold water to cover by 2 inches. Bring to a boil over medium-high heat; cook 15 minutes or until partially cooked. Drain potatoes; let stand until cool enough to handle. Cut into ½-inch-thick slices.

2. Cook bacon in large skillet over medium-high heat 6 to 7 minutes or until crisp, turning occasionally. Drain on paper towel-lined plate. Chop bacon; set aside.

3. Drain all but 2 tablespoons drippings from skillet; heat over medium heat. Add onions; cook 8 to 9 minutes or until softened but not browned, stirring occasionally. Transfer to small bowl.

4. Add butter to same skillet; heat over medium heat until melted. Add potatoes; sprinkle with salt and pepper. Top with onions and pour in ⅓ cup water; cover and cook 5 minutes. Stir in bacon; cook, uncovered, 10 to 12 minutes or until potatoes are tender and browned, stirring occasionally. *Makes 4 servings*

LEEK AND CHIVE CHAMP

3 medium russet potatoes (1½ pounds), peeled and cut into 1-inch pieces
6 tablespoons butter, divided
2 large leeks, white and light green parts only, halved and sliced
½ cup milk
¼ cup chopped fresh chives
½ teaspoon salt
¼ teaspoon black pepper
½ cup French fried onions (optional)

1. Place potatoes in large saucepan; add cold water to cover by 2 inches. Bring to a boil over medium-high heat; cook 16 to 18 minutes or until tender. Drain potatoes; return to saucepan.

2. Meanwhile, melt 2 tablespoons butter in small skillet over medium heat. Add leeks; cook 5 to 6 minutes or until tender, stirring occasionally.

3. Heat milk in small saucepan over medium-high heat until hot. Add 2 tablespoons butter; cook until melted. Pour milk mixture into saucepan with potatoes; mash until smooth. Stir in leeks, chives, salt and pepper; mix well.

4. Transfer potato mixture to serving bowl; make large indentation in center. Melt remaining 2 tablespoons butter; pour into indentation. Sprinkle with fried onions, if desired. *Makes 4 to 6 servings*

ROASTED PARSNIPS, CARROTS AND RED ONION

2 carrots, quartered lengthwise and cut into 2-inch-long pieces

2 parsnips, peeled, quartered lengthwise and cut into 2-inch-long pieces

¾ cup vertically sliced red onion (¼-inch slices)

2 tablespoons extra virgin olive oil

1 tablespoon balsamic vinegar

¼ teaspoon salt

⅛ teaspoon black pepper

1. Preheat oven to 425°F. Line large baking sheet with foil.

2. Combine carrots, parsnips, onion, oil, vinegar, salt and pepper in large bowl; toss to coat. Spread in single layer on prepared baking sheet.

3. Roast 25 minutes or until tender, stirring occasionally. *Makes 4 servings*

TIP: Choose parsnips that are firm, unblemished, and small or medium in size (about 8 inches long). Rinse and scrub parsnips with a vegetable brush to remove embedded soil.

SAUTÉED GARLIC POTATOES

2 pounds boiling potatoes, peeled and cut into 1-inch pieces

3 tablespoons FILIPPO BERIO® Olive Oil

6 cloves garlic, unpeeled

1 tablespoon lemon juice

1 tablespoon chopped fresh chives

1 tablespoon chopped fresh parsley

Salt and freshly ground black pepper

Place potatoes in large colander; rinse under cold running water. Drain well; pat dry. In large nonstick skillet, heat olive oil over medium heat until hot. Add potatoes in single layer. Cook, stirring and turning frequently, 10 minutes or until golden brown. Add garlic. Cover; reduce heat to low and cook very gently, shaking pan and stirring mixture occasionally, 15 to 20 minutes or until potatoes are tender when pierced with fork. Remove garlic; remove and discard skins. In small bowl, crush garlic; stir in lemon juice. Add to potatoes; mix well. Cook 1 to 2 minutes or until heated through. Transfer to serving dish; sprinkle with chives and parsley. Season to taste with salt and pepper. *Makes 4 servings*

Tangy Red Cabbage with Apples and Bacon

8 slices Irish or thick-cut bacon

1 large onion, sliced

½ small head red cabbage (1 pound), thinly sliced

1 tablespoon sugar

1 Granny Smith apple, peeled and sliced

2 tablespoons cider vinegar

½ teaspoon salt

¼ teaspoon black pepper

1. Heat large skillet over medium-high heat. Add bacon; cook 6 to 8 minutes or until crisp, turning occasionally. Drain on paper towel-lined plate. Coarsely chop bacon.

2. Drain all but 2 tablespoons drippings from skillet. Add onion; cook and stir over medium-high heat 2 to 3 minutes or until onion begins to soften. Add cabbage and sugar; cook and stir 4 to 5 minutes or until cabbage wilts. Stir in apple; cook 3 minutes or until crisp-tender. Stir in vinegar; cook 1 minute or until absorbed.

3. Stir in bacon, salt and pepper; cook 1 minute or until heated through. Serve hot or at room temperature. *Makes 4 servings*

PARSNIP PATTIES

1 pound parsnips, peeled and cut into ¾-inch pieces
4 tablespoons (½ stick) butter, divided
¼ cup chopped onion
¼ cup all-purpose flour
⅓ cup milk
2 teaspoons chopped fresh chives
   Salt and black pepper
¾ cup fresh bread crumbs
2 tablespoons vegetable oil

1. Pour 1 inch of water into medium saucepan; bring to a boil over high heat. Add parsnips; cover and cook 10 minutes or until fork-tender. Drain parsnips; place in large bowl. Coarsely mash with fork.

2. Melt 2 tablespoons butter in small skillet over medium-high heat. Add onion; cook and stir until translucent. Add flour; whisk until bubbly and lightly browned. Whisk in milk until thickened. Add to mashed parsnips; stir until well blended. Stir in chives; season with salt and pepper.

3. Shape parsnip mixture into four patties. Spread bread crumbs on plate; coat patties with bread crumbs. Place patties on waxed paper; refrigerate 2 hours.

4. Heat remaining 2 tablespoons butter and oil in large skillet over medium-high heat until butter is melted and bubbly. Add patties; cook 5 minutes per side or until browned. *Makes 4 servings*

Haggerty

8 slices bacon (about 8 ounces)

3 onions, thinly sliced

5 medium unpeeled red potatoes (about 1¼ pounds), very thinly sliced

1½ cups (6 ounces) shredded Irish Cheddar cheese, divided

2 tablespoons butter, divided

Salt and black pepper

1. Preheat oven to 375°F.

2. Cook bacon in large ovenproof skillet until crisp. Drain on paper towel-lined plate; crumble into medium bowl. Drain all but 1 tablespoon drippings from skillet.

3. Add onions to skillet; cook and stir over medium heat about 8 minutes or until translucent but not browned. Drain on paper towel-lined plate. Add to bowl with bacon; mix well.

4. Reserve ¼ cup cheese; set aside. Melt 1 tablespoon butter in same skillet or 8- to 9-inch baking dish. Arrange one quarter of potato slices to cover bottom of skillet. Season with salt and pepper. Top with one third of bacon-onion mixture; sprinkle with one third of remaining cheese. Repeat layers twice. Top with remaining one quarter of potato slices; dot with remaining 1 tablespoon butter.

5. Cover with foil and bake 50 minutes. Uncover and bake 10 minutes or until potatoes are tender. *Turn oven to broil.* Broil 2 to 3 minutes or until lightly browned. Sprinkle with reserved ¼ cup cheese. Serve warm.

Makes 6 to 8 servings

TIP: Use a mandolin to slice the potatoes very thin (about ⅛ inch). Thicker pieces may require a longer cooking time.

PUB FARE

EMERALD ISLE LAMB CHOPS

2 tablespoons vegetable or olive oil, divided
2 tablespoons coarse Dijon mustard
1 tablespoon Irish whiskey
1 tablespoon minced fresh rosemary
2 teaspoons minced garlic
6 lamb loin chops (about 4 ounces each)
½ teaspoon salt
½ teaspoon black pepper
¾ cup dry white wine
2 tablespoons black currant jam
1 to 2 tablespoons butter, cut into pieces

1. Combine 1 tablespoon oil, mustard, whiskey, rosemary and garlic in small bowl to form paste. Season lamb chops with salt and pepper; spread paste over both sides. Cover and marinate 30 minutes at room temperature or refrigerate 2 to 3 hours.

2. Heat remaining 1 tablespoon oil in large skillet over medium-high heat. Add lamb chops in single layer; cook 2 to 3 minutes per side or until desired doneness. Remove to plate; keep warm.

3. Drain excess fat from skillet. Add wine; cook and stir about 5 minutes, scraping up brown bits from bottom of skillet. Stir in jam until well blended. Remove from heat; stir in butter until melted. Serve sauce over lamb chops.

Makes 4 to 6 servings

MUSSELS STEAMED IN GUINNESS

5 tablespoons butter, divided
½ cup chopped shallots
2 stalks celery, chopped
1 medium carrot, chopped
8 sprigs fresh parsley
⅔ cup Guinness
2 pounds mussels, scrubbed and debearded
Crusty bread

1. Melt 1 tablespoon butter in large saucepan over medium-high heat. Add shallots, celery, carrot and parsley; cook and stir 2 to 3 minutes or until vegetables begin to soften.

2. Add Guinness; bring to a boil and cook 2 minutes. Add mussels; cover and return to a boil. Cook 4 to 5 minutes or until mussels open. Uncover and cook 1 minute.

3. Remove from heat; discard any unopened mussels. Stir in remaining 4 tablespoons butter. Serve immediately in bowls with bread.

Makes 4 appetizer or 2 main-dish servings

Split Pea Soup with Ham and Ale

1 tablespoon olive oil

1 cup chopped onion

½ cup chopped carrot

½ cup chopped celery

3 cloves garlic, minced

1 bay leaf

¼ teaspoon dried thyme

1 bottle (12 ounces) India Pale Ale

4 cups reduced-sodium chicken broth

1 package (16 ounces) green split peas, picked over and rinsed

1 pound smoked ham hocks

2 cups water

1. Heat oil in large saucepan or Dutch oven over medium heat. Add onion, carrot, celery, garlic, bay leaf and thyme; cook 4 to 5 minutes or until vegetables begin to soften, stirring occasionally. Add ale; bring to boil over medium-high heat. Cook 6 to 7 minutes or until beer is reduced by half.

2. Stir in broth, split peas, ham hocks and water; bring to a boil. Reduce heat to medium-low; cover and simmer about 1 hour or until peas are tender, stirring occasionally.

3. Remove ham hocks; let stand until cool enough to handle. Remove ham from hocks; chop meat and return to saucepan, discarding bones. Remove and discard bay leaf. *Makes 6 servings*

BEEF POT PIE

½ cup all-purpose flour

1 teaspoon salt, divided

½ teaspoon black pepper, divided

1½ pounds lean beef stew meat (1-inch pieces)

2 tablespoons olive oil

1 pound new red potatoes, cubed

2 cups baby carrots

1 cup frozen pearl onions, thawed

1 parsnip, peeled and cut into 1-inch pieces

1 cup Irish stout

¾ cup beef broth

1 teaspoon chopped fresh thyme *or* ½ teaspoon dried thyme

1 refrigerated pie crust (half of 15-ounce package)

1. Preheat oven to 350°F. Combine flour, ½ teaspoon salt and ¼ teaspoon pepper in large resealable food storage bag. Add beef; shake to coat.

2. Heat oil in large skillet over medium-high heat. Add beef; cook until browned on all sides. (Do not crowd beef; cook in batches, if necessary.) Transfer to 2½- to 3-quart casserole. Stir in potatoes, carrots, onions and parsnip.

3. Add stout, broth, thyme, remaining ½ teaspoon salt and ¼ teaspoon pepper to same skillet. Bring to a boil, scraping up browned bits from bottom of skillet. Pour into casserole; mix well.

4. Cover and bake 2½ to 3 hours or until beef is fork-tender, stirring once. Uncover and let stand at room temperature 15 minutes.

5. *Increase oven temperature to 425°F.* Place pie crust over casserole and press edges to seal. Cut slits in crust to vent. Bake 15 to 20 minutes or until crust is golden brown. Cool slightly before serving.   *Makes 4 to 6 servings*

INDIVIDUAL BEEF POT PIES: Instead of refrigerated pie crust, use 1 sheet puff pastry (half of 17-ounce package). Divide beef filling among six individual ovenproof serving dishes. Cut puff pastry to fit, press over moistened edges and crimp to seal. Brush tops with 1 lightly beaten egg yolk. Bake in preheated 400°F oven 15 to 20 minutes or until crust is puffed and golden.

Lamb in Dill Sauce

  2 large boiling potatoes, peeled and cut into 1-inch cubes
  ½ cup chopped onion
1½ teaspoons salt
  ½ teaspoon black pepper
  ½ teaspoon dried dill weed *or* 4 sprigs fresh dill
  1 bay leaf
  2 pounds lamb stew meat, cut into 1-inch cubes
  1 cup plus 3 tablespoons water, divided
  2 tablespoons all-purpose flour
  1 teaspoon sugar
  2 tablespoons lemon juice
    Fresh dill (optional)

Slow Cooker Directions

1. Layer potatoes, onion, salt, pepper, dried dill, bay leaf, lamb and 1 cup water in slow cooker. Cover; cook on LOW 6 to 8 hours.

2. Remove lamb and potatoes to bowl with slotted spoon; cover and keep warm. Remove and discard bay leaf.

3. Stir remaining 3 tablespoons water into flour in small bowl until smooth. Add ½ cup cooking liquid and sugar; mix well. Stir into slow cooker. Turn slow cooker to HIGH. Cook, uncovered, on HIGH 15 minutes or until thickened.

4. Stir in lemon juice. Return lamb and potatoes to slow cooker. Cover; cook on HIGH 15 minutes or until heated through. Garnish with fresh dill.

Makes 6 servings

PUB-STYLE FISH AND CHIPS

¾ cup all-purpose flour, plus additional for dusting fish
½ cup flat beer
  Vegetable oil
3 large or 4 medium russet potatoes
1 egg, separated
1 pound cod fillets
  Salt
  Prepared tartar sauce and lemon wedges

1. Combine ¾ cup flour, beer and 2 teaspoons oil in small bowl. Cover and refrigerate 30 minutes to 2 hours.

2. Peel and cut potatoes into ¾-inch sticks. Place in large bowl of cold water. Pour at least 2 inches of oil into deep heavy saucepan or deep fryer; heat over medium heat to 320°F. Drain and thoroughly dry potatoes. Fry in batches 3 minutes or until slightly softened but not browned. Drain on paper towel-lined plate.

3. Stir egg yolk into reserved flour mixture. Beat egg white in medium bowl with electric mixer at medium-high speed until soft peaks form. Fold egg white into flour mixture. Season batter with pinch of salt.

4. Preheat oven to 200°F. Heat oil to 365°F. Cut fish into pieces about 6 inches long and 2 to 3 inches wide. Remove any pin bones. Dust fish with flour; dip fish into batter, shaking off excess. Lower carefully into oil; cook 4 to 6 minutes or until batter is browned and fish is cooked through, turning once. Cook fish in batches; do not crowd pan. (Allow temperature of oil to return to 365°F between batches.) Drain on paper towel-lined plate; keep warm in oven.

5. Return potatoes to hot oil; cook in batches 5 minutes or until browned and crisp. Drain on paper towel-lined plate; sprinkle with salt. Serve fish with potatoes, tartar sauce and lemon wedges. *Makes 4 servings*

Sausage, Cabbage and Onions

2 tablespoons olive oil

1 pound pork sausage, cut in half lengthwise and cut diagonally
    into ¾-inch slices

1 onion, thinly sliced

2 teaspoons fennel seeds

1 teaspoon caraway seeds

1 clove garlic, minced

½ cup water

1 pound cabbage (6 cups or ½ head), thinly sliced

2 pounds (5 medium) red potatoes, cut into ¾-inch pieces

1 bottle (12 ounces) lager beer or ale

½ teaspoon salt

¼ teaspoon black pepper

1. Heat oil in large skillet over medium heat. Add sausage; cook 5 minutes or until browned. Remove to plate with slotted spoon.

2. Add onion, fennel seeds, caraway seeds and garlic to same skillet; cook and stir 2 to 3 minutes or until onion is translucent. Stir in ½ cup water, scraping up browned bits from bottom of skillet. Add cabbage and potatoes; cook 10 minutes or until cabbage is wilted, stirring occasionally.

3. Stir in beer; cover and cook over medium-low heat 15 minutes or until potatoes are tender. Add salt and pepper; cook over medium heat 15 minutes until beer has reduced to sauce consistency. Return sausage to skillet; cook until heated through. *Makes 6 servings*

LAMB AND VEGETABLE PIE

      2 tablespoons vegetable oil
  1½ pounds boneless leg of lamb, cut into 1-inch cubes
      3 medium russet potatoes (about 12 ounces), peeled and cut into 1-inch cubes
    16 frozen pearl onions (about 1 cup)
      1 cup frozen peas and carrots
      3 tablespoons all-purpose flour
  1½ cups reduced-sodium beef broth
      3 tablespoons chopped fresh parsley
      2 tablespoons tomato paste
      2 teaspoons Worcestershire sauce
     ½ teaspoon salt
     ¼ teaspoon black pepper
      1 refrigerated pie crust (half of 15-ounce package)
      1 egg, lightly beaten

1. Spray 9-inch baking dish or deep-dish pie plate with nonstick cooking spray. Heat oil in large saucepan over medium-high heat. Add half of lamb; cook 4 to 5 minutes or until browned, turning occasionally. Remove lamb to plate; repeat with remaining lamb.

2. Add potatoes, onions and peas and carrots to saucepan; cook 2 minutes, stirring occasionally. Stir in lamb and any accumulated juices; cook 2 minutes. Add flour; cook and stir 1 minute. Stir in broth, parsley, tomato paste, Worcestershire sauce, salt and pepper; bring to a boil. Reduce heat to medium-low; cover and simmer about 30 minutes or until lamb and potatoes are tender, stirring occasionally. Transfer mixture to prepared baking dish; let cool 20 minutes.

3. Preheat oven to 400°F. Top lamb mixture with pie crust; flute edge. Brush crust with egg; cut several small slits in crust with tip of knife.

4. Bake about 25 minutes or until crust is golden brown and filling is thick and bubbly. Cool 5 minutes before serving.   *Makes 4 to 6 servings*

GUINNESS BEEF STEW

     3 tablespoons vegetable oil, divided
     3 pounds boneless beef chuck roast, cut into 1-inch pieces
     2 medium onions, chopped
     2 stalks celery, chopped
     3 tablespoons all-purpose flour
     1 tablespoon *each* minced garlic and tomato paste
     2 teaspoons chopped fresh thyme
  1½ teaspoons salt
     ½ teaspoon black pepper
     1 bottle (about 11 ounces) Guinness
     1 cup reduced-sodium beef broth
     3 carrots, peeled and cut into 1-inch chunks
     4 small turnips (12 ounces), peeled and cut into 1-inch pieces
     4 medium Yukon Gold potatoes (1 pound), peeled and cut into 1-inch pieces
     ¼ cup finely chopped fresh parsley

1. Preheat oven to 350°F. Heat 2 tablespoons oil in Dutch oven over medium-high heat until almost smoking. Cook beef in two batches about 10 minutes or until browned on all sides. Remove beef to large plate.

2. Add remaining 1 tablespoon oil to Dutch oven; heat over medium heat. Add onions and celery; cook about 8 minutes or until onions are softened and translucent. Add flour, garlic, tomato paste, thyme, salt and pepper; cook and stir 1 minute. Add Guinness; use wooden spoon to scrape up browned bits from bottom of Dutch oven. Return beef to pan; stir in broth.

3. Cover and bake 1 hour. Stir in carrots, turnips and potatoes; cover and bake about 1 hour 20 minutes or until beef and vegetables are tender. Stir in parsley.

Makes 6 servings

HAM WITH DARK BEER GRAVY

1 fully cooked bone-in ham (about 6 pounds)
1 tablespoon Dijon mustard
2 cans (6 ounces each) pineapple juice
1 bottle (12 ounces) porter or stout
   Dark Beer Gravy (recipe follows)

1. Line large roasting pan with foil.

2. Remove skin and excess fat from ham. Score ham in diamond pattern.

3. Place ham in prepared pan. Spread mustard over ham. Pour pineapple juice and beer over ham. Cover and refrigerate 8 hours.

4. Preheat oven to 350°F. Cook ham 1½ hours or until 140°F, basting every 30 minutes. Remove to cutting board; cover and let stand 15 minutes before slicing.

5. Meanwhile, pour drippings from roasting pan into 4-cup measuring cup. Let stand 5 minutes; skim and discard fat. Prepare Dark Beer Gravy; serve with ham.   *Makes 10 to 12 servings*

DARK BEER GRAVY: Melt ¼ cup (½ stick) butter in small saucepan over medium heat. Whisk in ¼ cup all-purpose flour until blended. Cook 1 to 2 minutes, whisking constantly. Add ½ cup dark beer (such as porter) to 2 cups ham drippings; whisk into flour mixture. Cook until mixture is thickened and bubbly, whisking constantly. Season with salt and black pepper.

LAMB AND MINT HAND PIES

2 cups plus 1 tablespoon all-purpose flour, divided

1 teaspoon salt, divided

10 tablespoons cold butter, cut into small pieces

7 to 8 tablespoons ice water

1 pound ground lamb

1 small onion, finely chopped

1 carrot, finely chopped

½ cup reduced-sodium beef broth

1 teaspoon Dijon mustard

¼ teaspoon black pepper

1 tablespoon chopped fresh mint

½ cup (2 ounces) shredded Irish Cheddar cheese

1 egg, lightly beaten

1. For dough, combine 2 cups flour and ½ teaspoon salt in medium bowl. Cut in butter with pastry blender or two knives until mixture resembles coarse crumbs. Add water, 1 tablespoon at a time, stirring with fork until loose dough forms. Knead dough in bowl 1 to 2 times until it comes together. Divide dough into four pieces; press each into 4-inch disc. Wrap dough in plastic wrap; freeze 15 minutes.

2. Meanwhile, prepare filling. Heat large skillet over medium-high heat. Add lamb; cook 7 to 8 minutes or until lightly browned, stirring occasionally. Drain well; remove to plate. Add onion and carrot to skillet; cook 3 minutes or until vegetables begin to soften, stirring occasionally. Stir in lamb; cook 1 minute. Add remaining 1 tablespoon flour; cook and stir 1 minute. Add broth, mustard, remaining ½ teaspoon salt and pepper; cook over medium heat about 2 minutes or until thickened. Remove from heat; stir in mint. Cool 10 minutes. Stir in cheese.

3. Position rack in center of oven. Preheat oven to 400°F. Line large baking sheet with parchment paper or spray with nonstick cooking spray.

4. Working with one disc at a time, roll out dough into 9-inch circle on lightly floured surface. Cut out four circles with 4-inch round cookie cutter (16 circles total). Place 8 dough circles on prepared baking sheet. Top each with ⅛ of lamb filling, leaving ½-inch border around edge of circle. Top with remaining dough circles, pressing edges to seal. Press edges again with tines of fork. Brush tops with egg; cut 1-inch slit in top of each pie with tip of knife.

5. Bake 28 to 30 minutes or until golden brown. Serve hot or at room temperature.

Makes 4 main-dish or 8 appetizer servings

Roasted Garlic and Stout Mac and Cheese

1 head garlic
1 tablespoon olive oil
6 tablespoons butter, divided
1 cup panko bread crumbs
1¼ teaspoons salt, divided
¼ cup all-purpose flour
½ teaspoon black pepper
2 cups whole milk
¾ cup Irish stout
2 cups (8 ounces) shredded sharp Cheddar cheese
2 cups (8 ounces) shredded Dubliner cheese
1 pound cellentani, rotini or penne pasta, cooked and drained

1. Preheat oven to 375°F. Spray 4-quart shallow baking dish with nonstick cooking spray. Place garlic on 10-inch piece of foil; drizzle with oil and crimp shut. Place on small baking sheet; bake 30 minutes or until tender. Cool 15 minutes; squeeze cloves into small bowl. Mash into smooth paste.

2. Microwave 2 tablespoons butter in medium bowl until melted. Stir in panko and ¼ teaspoon salt until well blended.

3. Melt remaining 4 tablespoons butter in large saucepan over medium heat. Add flour; cook and stir until light brown. Stir in roasted garlic paste, remaining 1 teaspoon salt and pepper. Slowly whisk in milk and stout. Simmer until thickened, whisking constantly. Remove from heat; whisk in cheeses, ½ cup at a time, until melted. Combine cheese mixture and pasta in large bowl. Transfer to prepared baking dish; sprinkle with panko mixture.

4. Bake 40 minutes or until bubbly and topping is golden brown. Let stand 10 minutes before serving.

Makes 8 to 10 servings

BLUE CHEESE-STUFFED SIRLOIN PATTIES

1½ pounds ground beef sirloin
½ cup (2 ounces) shredded sharp Cheddar cheese
¼ cup crumbled blue cheese
¼ cup finely chopped parsley
2 teaspoons Dijon mustard
1 teaspoon Worcestershire sauce
1 clove garlic, minced
½ teaspoon salt, divided
2 teaspoons olive oil
1 medium red bell pepper, cut into thin strips

1. Shape beef into eight patties, about 4 inches in diameter and ¼ inch thick.

2. Combine Cheddar cheese, blue cheese, parsley, mustard, Worcestershire sauce, garlic and ¼ teaspoon salt in small bowl; toss gently to blend.

3. Top each of four patties with one fourth of cheese mixture (about 3 tablespoons). Top with remaining four patties; pinch edges to seal.

4. Heat oil in large skillet over medium-high heat until hot. Add bell pepper; cook and stir until edges begin to brown. Sprinkle with remaining ¼ teaspoon salt. Remove from skillet; cover to keep warm.

5. Add beef patties to same skillet; cook over medium-high heat 5 minutes. Turn patties; top with peppers. Cook 4 minutes or until medium (160°F) or until desired doneness.   *Makes 4 servings*

SHEPHERD'S PIE

3 medium russet potatoes (1½ pounds), peeled and cut into 1-inch pieces
½ cup milk
5 tablespoons butter, divided
1 teaspoon salt, divided
½ teaspoon black pepper, divided
2 medium onions, chopped
2 medium carrots, finely chopped
½ teaspoon dried thyme
1½ pounds ground lamb
3 tablespoons tomato paste
1 tablespoon Worcestershire sauce
1½ cups reduced-sodium beef broth
½ cup frozen peas

1. Preheat oven to 350°F. Spray 1½-quart baking dish with nonstick cooking spray.

2. Place potatoes in large saucepan; add cold water to cover by 2 inches. Bring to a boil over medium-high heat; cook 16 to 18 minutes or until tender. Drain potatoes; return to saucepan.

3. Heat milk in small saucepan over medium-high heat until hot. Add 3 tablespoons butter, ½ teaspoon salt and ¼ teaspoon pepper; stir until butter is melted. Pour milk mixture into saucepan with potatoes; mash until smooth. Set aside.

4. Melt remaining 2 tablespoons butter in large skillet over medium heat. Add onions, carrots and thyme; cook 8 to 10 minutes until vegetables are softened but not browned, stirring occasionally. Add lamb; cook over medium-high heat 4 minutes or until no longer pink. Drain excess fat. Return skillet to heat; cook about 5 minutes or until lamb is lightly browned. Add tomato paste and Worcestershire sauce; cook 1 minute. Stir in broth; bring to a boil and cook

7 minutes or until nearly evaporated. Stir in peas, remaining ½ teaspoon salt and ¼ teaspoon pepper; cook 30 seconds. Transfer mixture to prepared baking dish.

5. Spread mashed potatoes in even layer over lamb mixture; use spatula to swirl potatoes or fork to make crosshatch design on top.

6. Bake about 35 minutes or until filling is hot and bubbly and potatoes begin to brown. *Makes 4 to 6 servings*

LAMB SHANKS BRAISED IN STOUT

4 lamb shanks (about 1 pound each)*
¼ cup all-purpose flour
¼ cup vegetable oil, plus additional as needed
1 large onion, chopped (about 2 cups)
4 cloves garlic, minced
   Salt and black pepper
3 sprigs fresh rosemary
3 sprigs fresh thyme
1 bottle (about 11 ounces) Irish stout
2 to 3 cups reduced-sodium chicken broth
   Smashed Chat Potatoes (recipe follows)
1 tablespoon chopped fresh mint

*For a more attractive presentation, ask butcher to "french" chops by removing flesh from last inch of bone end.

1. Preheat oven to 325°F. Trim excess fat from lamb. (Do not remove all fat or shanks will fall apart while cooking.) Dust lamb shanks with flour. Heat ¼ cup oil in Dutch oven or large roasting pan over medium-high heat. Add lamb in batches; cook until browned on all sides. Remove to bowl.

2. Add oil to pan, if necessary, to make about 2 tablespoons. Add onion; cook and stir 2 minutes. Add garlic; cook and stir 2 minutes. Return lamb shanks and any accumulated juices to pan. Sprinkle generously with salt and pepper. Tuck rosemary and thyme sprigs around lamb. Add stout to pan; pour in broth to almost cover lamb.

3. Cover and bake 2 hours or until lamb is very tender and almost falling off bones. Prepare Smashed Chat Potatoes.

4. Remove lamb shanks to plate; keep warm. Skim fat from juices in pan; boil until reduced by half. Strain sauce. Serve lamb over potatoes; sprinkle with mint.

Makes 4 servings

SMASHED CHAT POTATOES: Place 1½ to 2 pounds unpeeled small white potatoes in large saucepan; add cold water to cover by 2 inches. Bring to a boil over high heat. Reduce heat to medium-low; simmer about 20 minutes or until fork-tender. Drain potatoes; return to saucepan and stir in 1 tablespoon butter until melted. Partially smash potatoes with fork or potato masher. Season with salt and black pepper.

CHEESE AND BEER FONDUE

¾ **cup lager**
1 **teaspoon mustard**
¼ **teaspoon Worcestershire sauce**
⅛ **teaspoon ground red pepper**
2 **cups (8 ounces) shredded sharp Cheddar cheese**
4½ **teaspoons all-purpose flour**
  Sliced French bread

1. Whisk beer, mustard, Worcestershire sauce and red pepper in large saucepan; bring to a boil over high heat. Reduce heat to medium-low.

2. Toss cheese with flour in medium bowl. Whisk into beer mixture, 1 cup at a time, whisking after each addition until smooth. Gently boil 2 minutes, stirring constantly. Serve with bread. *Makes about 6 servings*

SERVING TIPS: To serve from fondue pot, prepare as directed above. Transfer to preheated fondue pot after boiling for 2 minutes as directed in step 2. The fondue can also be transferred to small (2-quart or smaller) slow cooker set on LOW.

DUBLIN CODDLE

½ pound fresh brussels sprouts

2 pounds potatoes, peeled and cut into ½-inch-thick slices

1 pound Irish pork sausage,* cut into 1-inch slices

1 pound smoked ham, cut into cubes

3 onions, cut into 1-inch pieces

8 ounces baby carrots

1 teaspoon dried thyme

½ teaspoon black pepper

*Irish pork sausage is similar to fresh garlic-flavored bratwurst. If unavailable, substitute 1 pound regular pork sausage and add 1 clove minced garlic with ingredients in step 2.

1. Cut stem from each brussels sprout and pull off outer bruised leaves. Cut deep "X" into stem end of each sprout with paring knife.

2. Combine potatoes, sausage, ham, brussels sprouts, onions, carrots, thyme and pepper in large saucepan or Dutch oven. Add enough water to cover; bring to a boil over high heat. Reduce heat to medium; cover and simmer 20 minutes. Uncover and cook 15 minutes or until vegetables are tender.

3. Cool slightly. Skim any fat from surface of liquid before serving.

Makes 8 to 10 servings

~ BREADS ~

Irish Soda Bread

2½ cups all-purpose flour
1¼ cups whole wheat flour
  1 cup currants
  ¼ cup sugar
  4 teaspoons baking powder
  2 teaspoons caraway seeds (optional)
  1 teaspoon salt
  ½ teaspoon baking soda
  ½ cup (1 stick) butter, cut into small pieces
1⅓ to 1½ cups buttermilk

1. Preheat oven to 350°F. Line baking sheet with parchment paper.

2. Combine all-purpose flour, whole wheat flour, currants, sugar, baking powder, caraway seeds, if desired, salt and baking soda in large bowl.

3. Cut in butter with pastry blender or two knives until mixture resembles coarse crumbs. Add buttermilk; mix until slightly sticky dough forms. Place dough on prepared baking sheet; shape into 8-inch round.

4. Bake 50 to 60 minutes or until bread is golden and crust is firm. Cool on baking sheet 10 minutes; remove to wire rack to cool completely.

Makes 12 servings

HONEY SCONES

2 cups all-purpose flour
½ cup old-fashioned oats
2 tablespoons packed brown sugar
1 tablespoon granulated sugar
1 tablespoon baking powder
½ teaspoon salt
6 tablespoons butter, melted
¼ cup whipping cream
¼ cup milk
1 egg
3 tablespoons honey

1. Preheat oven to 425°F. Line baking sheet with parchment paper.

2. Combine flour, oats, brown sugar, granulated sugar, baking powder and salt in large bowl. Whisk butter, cream, milk, egg and honey in medium bowl until well blended. Add to flour mixture; stir just until dough comes together.

3. Turn dough out onto lightly floured surface. Pat dough into 8-inch round, about ¾ inch thick. Cut into eight triangles; place 1 to 2 inches apart on prepared baking sheet.

4. Bake 12 to 15 minutes until golden brown. Remove to wire rack to cool 15 minutes. Serve warm. *Makes 8 scones*

BEER AND BACON MUFFINS

6 slices bacon, chopped
2 cups chopped onions
3 teaspoons sugar, divided
¼ teaspoon dried thyme
1½ cups all-purpose flour
¾ cup grated Parmesan cheese
2 teaspoons baking powder
½ teaspoon salt
¾ cup lager or other light-colored beer
2 eggs
¼ cup extra virgin olive oil

1. Preheat oven to 375°F. Spray 12 standard (2½-inch) muffin cups with nonstick cooking spray.

2. Cook bacon in large skillet over medium heat until crisp, stirring occasionally. Remove bacon to paper towel-lined plate with slotted spoon. Add onions, 1 teaspoon sugar and thyme to skillet; cook 12 minutes or until onions are golden brown, stirring occasionally. Cool 5 minutes; stir in bacon.

3. Combine flour, cheese, baking powder, salt and remaining 2 teaspoons sugar in large bowl. Whisk lager, eggs and oil in medium bowl. Add to flour mixture; stir just until moistened. Gently stir in onion mixture. Spoon batter evenly into prepared muffin cups.

4. Bake 15 minutes or until toothpick inserted into centers comes out clean. Cool in pan on wire rack 5 minutes. Serve warm or cool completely.

Makes 12 servings

Barm Brack

4 to 4½ cups all-purpose flour
½ cup plus 1 teaspoon sugar, divided
1 package (¼ ounce) rapid-rise active dry yeast
1 teaspoon salt
½ teaspoon ground cinnamon
¼ teaspoon ground nutmeg
¾ cup plus 1 tablespoon water, divided
¾ cup milk
¼ cup (½ stick) butter, softened
1 egg
1 cup golden raisins (optional)
½ cup chopped dried or candied fruit (apricots, cherries, prunes, etc.)

1. Place 4 cups flour in large bowl. Stir in ½ cup sugar, yeast, salt, cinnamon and nutmeg. Combine ¾ cup water, milk and butter in small saucepan; heat over low heat until butter melts and temperature reaches 120° to 130°F. Add to flour mixture; beat with electric mixer at medium speed 2 minutes or until well blended. Beat in egg.

2. Gradually add additional flour until slightly sticky dough forms. Attach dough hook to mixer; knead at low speed 4 minutes or knead 8 minutes by hand on lightly floured surface. Place dough in greased bowl; turn to grease top. Cover and let rise in warm place 45 minutes to 1 hour or until doubled in size.

3. Spray two 8×4-inch loaf pans with nonstick cooking spray. Punch down dough; turn out onto floured surface. Knead in raisins, if desired, and dried fruit. Divide dough into two balls; cover and let rest 5 minutes. To shape loaves, flatten and stretch each ball of dough into oval shape. Bring long sides together and pinch to seal; fold over short ends and pinch to seal. Place seam side down in prepared pans. Cover and let rise 45 minutes or until dough almost reaches tops of pans.

4. Preheat oven to 375°F. Bake 35 to 40 minutes or until browned. (Cover loosely with foil if loaves begin to overbrown.) Dissolve remaining 1 teaspoon sugar in 1 tablespoon water in small bowl. Brush over loaves; bake 2 minutes. Cool in pans 2 minutes; remove to wire rack to cool slightly. Serve warm. *Makes 2 loaves*

Irish-Style Scones

2 cups all-purpose flour

2 teaspoons baking powder

¼ teaspoon salt

¼ cup (½ stick) cold butter, cut into small pieces

¼ cup finely chopped pitted dates

¼ cup golden raisins or currants

3 eggs, divided

½ cup whipping cream

1½ teaspoons vanilla

1 teaspoon water

   Orange marmalade fruit spread

   Whipped cream or crème fraîche

1. Preheat oven to 375°F. Line baking sheet with parchment paper.

2. Combine flour, baking powder and salt in medium bowl. Cut in butter with pastry blender or two knives until mixture resembles coarse crumbs. Stir in dates and raisins. Whisk 2 eggs, cream and vanilla in medium bowl until well blended. Add to flour mixture; stir just until moistened.

3. Turn out dough onto lightly floured surface; knead dough four times with floured hands. Place dough on prepared baking sheet; pat into 8-inch circle. Gently score dough into six wedges with sharp wet knife, cutting three-fourths of the way through dough. Beat remaining egg and water in small bowl; brush lightly over dough.

4. Bake 18 to 20 minutes or until golden brown. Remove to wire rack to cool 5 minutes. Cut into wedges; serve warm with marmalade and whipped cream.

Makes 6 scones

BUTTERMILK BISCUITS

2 cups all-purpose flour
1 tablespoon baking powder
2 teaspoons sugar
½ teaspoon salt
½ teaspoon baking soda
⅓ cup shortening
⅔ cup buttermilk*

Or substitute soured fresh milk. To sour milk, combine 2½ teaspoons lemon juice plus enough milk to equal ⅔ cup. Stir; let stand 5 minutes before using.

1. Preheat oven to 450°F.

2. Combine flour, baking powder, sugar, salt and baking soda in medium bowl. Cut in shortening with pastry blender or two knives until mixture resembles coarse crumbs. Make well in center of dry ingredients. Add buttermilk; stir until mixture forms soft dough that clings together and forms a ball.

3. Turn out dough onto well-floured surface; knead gently 10 to 12 times. Roll or pat dough to ½-inch thickness. Cut out dough with floured 2½-inch biscuit cutter. Place 2 inches apart on ungreased baking sheet.

4. Bake 8 to 10 minutes or until golden brown. Serve warm.

Makes about 9 biscuits

DROP BISCUITS: Prepare Buttermilk Biscuits as directed in step 2, increasing buttermilk to 1 cup. Stir batter with wooden spoon about 15 strokes. *Do not knead.* Drop dough by heaping tablespoonfuls 1 inch apart onto greased baking sheet. Bake as directed in step 4. Makes about 18 biscuits.

Oatmeal Honey Bread

1½ to 2 cups all-purpose flour
 1 cup plus 1 tablespoon old-fashioned oats, divided
 ½ cup whole wheat flour
 1 package (¼ ounce) rapid-rise active dry yeast
 1 teaspoon salt
1⅓ cups plus 1 tablespoon water, divided
 ¼ cup honey
 2 tablespoons butter
 1 egg

1. Combine 1½ cups all-purpose flour, 1 cup oats, whole wheat flour, yeast and salt in large bowl.

2. Heat 1⅓ cups water, honey and butter in small saucepan over low heat until honey dissolves and butter melts. Let cool to 130°F (temperature of very hot tap water). Add to flour mixture; beat with electric mixer at medium speed 2 minutes. Add additional flour by tablespoonfuls until dough begins to cling together. Dough should be shaggy and very sticky, not dry. (Dough should not form a ball and/or clean side of bowl.)

3. Attach dough hook to mixer; knead at medium-low speed 4 minutes. Place dough in greased bowl; turn to grease top. Cover and let rise in warm place 45 minutes or until doubled in size.

4. Spray 8×4-inch loaf pan with nonstick cooking spray. Punch down dough; turn out onto floured surface. Flatten and stretch dough into 8-inch-long oval. Bring long sides together and pinch to seal; fold over short ends and pinch to seal. Place dough seam side down in prepared pan. Cover and let rise in warm place 20 to 30 minutes or until dough reaches top of pan.

5. Preheat oven to 375°F. Beat egg and remaining 1 tablespoon water in small bowl. Brush top of loaf with egg mixture; sprinkle with remaining 1 tablespoon oats. Bake 30 to 35 minutes or until bread sounds hollow when tapped. Remove to wire rack to cool completely.   *Makes 1 loaf*

ORANGE-CURRANT SCONES

1½ cups all-purpose flour
¼ cup plus 1 teaspoon sugar, divided
1 teaspoon baking powder
¼ teaspoon baking soda
¼ teaspoon salt
⅓ cup currants
1 tablespoon grated orange peel
6 tablespoons cold butter, cut into small pieces
½ cup buttermilk, yogurt or sour cream

1. Preheat oven to 425°F. Line baking sheet with parchment paper.

2. Combine flour, ¼ cup sugar, baking powder, baking soda and salt in large bowl. Stir in currants and orange peel. Cut in butter with pastry blender or two knives until mixture resembles coarse crumbs. Add buttermilk; stir until mixture forms soft sticky dough that clings together.

3. Shape dough into a ball; pat into 8-inch round on prepared baking sheet. Cut dough into eight wedges with floured knife. Sprinkle with remaining 1 teaspoon sugar.

4. Bake 18 to 20 minutes or until golden brown. Remove to wire rack to cool 5 minutes. Serve warm. *Makes 8 scones*

Treacle Bread
(Brown Soda Bread)

2 cups all-purpose flour

1 cup whole wheat flour

1 teaspoon baking soda

½ teaspoon salt

½ teaspoon ground ginger

1¼ cups buttermilk, plus additional as needed

3 tablespoons dark molasses (preferably blackstrap)

1. Preheat oven to 375°F. Line baking sheet with parchment paper.

2. Combine all-purpose flour, whole wheat flour, baking soda, salt and ginger in large bowl. Combine 1¼ cups buttermilk and molasses in small bowl; mix well.

3. Stir buttermilk mixture into flour mixture. Add additional buttermilk by tablespoonfuls if needed to make dry, rough dough. Turn out dough onto floured surface; knead 8 to 10 times or just until smooth. (Do not overknead.) Shape dough into round loaf about 1½ inches thick. Place on prepared baking sheet.

4. Use floured knife to cut halfway through dough, scoring into quarters (called farls in Ireland). Sprinkle top of dough with additional flour, if desired.

5. Bake about 35 minutes or until bread sounds hollow when tapped. Remove to wire rack to cool slightly. Serve warm. *Makes 6 to 8 servings*

NOTE: Treacle Bread can be sliced or pulled apart into farls.

Quaker's Best Oatmeal Bread

5¾ to 6¼ cups all-purpose flour

2½ cups QUAKER® Oats (quick or old fashioned, uncooked)

¼ cup granulated sugar

2 packages (¼ ounce each) quick-rising yeast (about 4½ teaspoons)

2½ teaspoons salt

1½ cups water

1¼ cups fat-free (skim) milk

¼ cup (½ stick) margarine or butter

1. Combine 3 cups flour, oats, sugar, yeast and salt in large bowl; mix well. Heat water, milk and margarine in small saucepan until very warm (120°F to 130°F). Add to flour mixture. Blend with electric mixer at low speed until dry ingredients are moistened. Increase to medium speed; beat 3 minutes. By hand, gradually stir in enough remaining flour to make stiff dough.

2. Turn dough out onto lightly floured surface. Knead 5 to 8 minutes or until smooth and elastic. Shape dough into ball; place in greased bowl, turning once. Cover; let rise in warm place 30 minutes or until doubled in size.

3. Punch down dough. Cover; let rest 10 minutes. Divide dough in half; shape to form loaves. Place in two greased 8×4-inch or 9×5-inch loaf pans. Cover; let rise in warm place 15 minutes or until nearly doubled in size.

4. Heat oven to 375°F. Bake 45 to 50 minutes or until dark golden brown. Remove from pans to wire rack. Cool completely before slicing.

Makes 2 loaves (32 servings)

Tip: If desired, brush tops of loaves lightly with melted margarine or butter and sprinkle with additional oats after placing in pans.

OAT AND WHOLE WHEAT SCONES

1 cup old-fashioned oats
1 cup whole wheat flour
½ cup all-purpose flour
¼ cup sugar
1 tablespoon baking powder
¼ teaspoon salt
½ cup (1 stick) butter, cut into small pieces
½ cup whipping cream
1 egg
¾ cup dried cherries

1. Preheat oven to 425°F. Line baking sheet with parchment paper.

2. Combine oats, whole wheat flour, all-purpose flour, sugar, baking powder and salt in large bowl. Cut in butter with pastry blender or two forks until mixture resembles coarse crumbs.

3. Whisk cream and egg in small bowl until well blended. Add to flour mixture; stir just until dough comes together. Stir in cherries.

4. Turn out dough onto lightly floured surface. Shape dough into 8-inch disc about ¾ inch thick. Cut into eight wedges; place 1 inch apart on prepared baking sheet.

5. Bake about 15 minutes or until golden brown. Remove to wire rack to cool 5 minutes. Serve warm.

Makes 8 scones

DESSERTS

Bread and Butter Pudding

3 tablespoons butter, softened
1 pound egg bread or firm white bread, sliced
⅔ cup golden raisins
¾ cup sugar, divided
1 teaspoon ground cinnamon
¼ teaspoon ground nutmeg
2 cups half-and-half
2 cups whole milk
6 eggs
1½ teaspoons vanilla

1. Preheat oven to 350°F. Spray 1½-quart or 13×9-inch baking dish with nonstick cooking spray.

2. Lightly butter both sides of bread slices. Cut into 1½-inch pieces. Combine bread and raisins in prepared baking dish. Combine ¼ cup sugar, cinnamon and nutmeg in small bowl; sprinkle over bread mixture and toss to coat.

3. Whisk half-and-half, milk, eggs, remaining ½ cup sugar and vanilla in large bowl until well blended. Pour over bread mixture; let stand 10 minutes.

4. Bake about 1 hour or until pudding is set, puffed and golden brown. Serve warm or at room temperature. *Makes 8 to 10 servings*

IRISH SODA BREAD COOKIES

2 cups all-purpose flour
½ teaspoon baking soda
¼ teaspoon salt
½ cup (1 stick) butter, softened
½ cup sugar
1 egg
¾ cup currants
1 teaspoon caraway seeds
⅓ cup buttermilk

1. Preheat oven to 350°F. Line cookie sheets with parchment paper.

2. Combine flour, baking soda and salt in medium bowl. Beat butter and sugar in large bowl with electric mixer at medium speed until light and fluffy. Add egg; beat 1 minute or until blended. Add flour mixture; beat at low speed until blended. Beat in currants and caraway seeds. Add buttermilk; beat until blended. Drop tablespoonfuls of dough 1 inch apart on prepared cookie sheets.

3. Bake 12 to 15 minutes or until golden brown. Remove to wire racks to cool slightly. Serve warm. *Makes about 3 dozen cookies*

APPLE-BUTTERMILK PIE

  2 medium Granny Smith apples
  3 eggs
1½ cups sugar, divided
  1 cup buttermilk
  ⅓ cup butter, melted
  2 tablespoons all-purpose flour
  2 teaspoons ground cinnamon, divided
  2 teaspoons vanilla
  ¾ teaspoon ground nutmeg, divided
  1 (9-inch) unbaked pie shell
    Whipped cream and additional ground cinnamon (optional)

1. Preheat oven to 350°F. Peel and core apples; cut into small pieces. Place apples in small bowl; cover with cold water.

2. Beat eggs in medium bowl with electric mixer at low speed until blended. Add all but 1 teaspoon sugar, buttermilk, butter, flour, 1 teaspoon cinnamon, vanilla and ½ teaspoon nutmeg; beat at low speed until well blended.

3. Drain apples well; place in unbaked pie shell. Pour buttermilk mixture over apples. Combine remaining 1 teaspoon sugar, 1 teaspoon cinnamon and ¼ teaspoon nutmeg in small bowl; sprinkle over top.

4. Bake 50 to 60 minutes or until knife inserted into center comes out clean. Serve warm or at room temperature. Garnish with whipped cream and additional cinnamon. *Makes 6 to 8 servings*

Ginger Stout Cake

2 cups all-purpose flour

2 teaspoons ground ginger

1½ teaspoons baking powder

1½ teaspoons baking soda

¾ teaspoon ground cinnamon, plus additional for garnish

½ teaspoon salt

¼ teaspoon ground cloves

½ cup (1 stick) butter, softened

1 tablespoon grated fresh ginger *or* 1 teaspoon ground ginger

1 cup granulated sugar

½ cup packed brown sugar

3 eggs

1 bottle (11 ounces) Irish stout

½ cup molasses

Whipped cream (optional)

1. Preheat oven to 350°F. Spray 13×9-inch baking pan with nonstick cooking spray. Combine flour, ground ginger, baking powder, baking soda, ¾ teaspoon cinnamon, salt and cloves in medium bowl.

2. Beat butter and grated ginger in large bowl with electric mixer at medium speed until creamy. Add granulated sugar and brown sugar; beat until light and fluffy. Add eggs, one at a time, beating well after each addition. Combine stout and molasses in small bowl. Alternately add flour mixture and stout mixture to butter mixture, beating well after each addition. Pour batter into prepared pan.

3. Bake 45 minutes or until toothpick inserted into center comes out clean. Cool completely in pan on wire rack. Garnish with whipped cream and additional cinnamon. *Makes 12 to 15 servings*

Lemon Tart

1 refrigerated pie crust (half of 15-ounce package)
5 eggs
1 tablespoon cornstarch
1 cup sugar
½ cup (1 stick) butter
½ cup lemon juice

1. Position rack in center of oven. Preheat oven to 450°F.

2. Line 9-inch tart pan with pie crust, pressing to fit securely against side of pan. Trim off any excess crust. Prick bottom and side of crust with fork. Bake 9 to 10 minutes or until golden brown. Cool completely. *Reduce oven temperature to 350°F.*

3. Meanwhile, whisk eggs and cornstarch in medium bowl. Combine sugar, butter and lemon juice in small saucepan; cook and stir over medium-low heat just until butter melts. Whisk in egg mixture; cook 8 to 10 minutes or until thickened, stirring constantly. (Do not let mixture come to a boil.) Pour into medium bowl; stir 1 minute or until cooled slightly. Let cool 10 minutes.

4. Pour cooled lemon curd into baked crust. Bake 25 to 30 minutes or until set. Cool completely before cutting. Store leftovers in refrigerator.

Makes 8 to 10 servings

STRAWBERRY RHUBARB PIE

Double-Crust Pie Pastry (recipe follows)
1½ cups sugar
½ cup cornstarch
2 tablespoons quick-cooking tapioca
1 tablespoon grated lemon peel
¼ teaspoon ground allspice
4 cups sliced rhubarb (1-inch pieces)
3 cups sliced fresh strawberries
1 egg, lightly beaten

1. Prepare Double-Crust Pie Pastry.

2. Preheat oven to 425°F. Roll out one pastry disc into 11-inch circle on floured surface. Line 9-inch pie plate with pastry.

3. Combine sugar, cornstarch, tapioca, lemon peel and allspice in large bowl. Add rhubarb and strawberries; toss to coat. Pour into crust. (Do not mound in center.)

4. Roll out remaining pastry disc into 10-inch circle. Cut into ½-inch-wide strips. Arrange in lattice design over filling; seal and flute edge. Brush pastry with beaten egg.

5. Bake 50 minutes or until pastry is golden brown and filling is thick and bubbly. Cool on wire rack. Serve warm or at room temperature.   *Makes 8 servings*

DOUBLE-CRUST PIE PASTRY: Combine 2½ cups all-purpose flour, 1 teaspoon salt and 1 teaspoon sugar in large bowl. Cut in 1 cup (2 sticks) cold cubed butter with pastry blender or two knives until mixture resembles coarse crumbs. Drizzle ⅓ cup water over flour mixture, 2 tablespoons at a time, stirring just until dough comes together. Divide dough in half. Shape each half into disc; wrap with plastic wrap. Refrigerate 30 minutes.

RHUBARB TART

  1 refrigerated pie crust (half of 15-ounce package)
  4 cups sliced rhubarb (½-inch pieces)
1¼ cups sugar
  ¼ cup all-purpose flour
  2 tablespoons butter, cut into pieces
  ¼ cup old-fashioned oats

1. Preheat oven to 450°F. Line 9-inch pie plate with crust. Trim excess crust; flute or crimp edge.

2. Combine rhubarb, sugar and flour in medium bowl; pour into pie crust. Dot with butter; sprinkle with oats.

3. Bake 10 minutes. *Reduce oven temperature to 350°F.* Bake 40 minutes or until bubbly.   *Makes 8 servings*

IRISH COFFEE

6 ounces freshly brewed strong black coffee
2 teaspoons packed brown sugar
2 ounces Irish whiskey
¼ cup whipping cream

Combine coffee and brown sugar in Irish coffee glass or mug. Stir in whiskey. Pour cream over back of spoon into coffee.   *Makes 1 serving*

Rhubarb Tart

APPLE BLACKBERRY CRISP

4 cups sliced apples
Juice of ½ lemon
2 tablespoons granulated sugar
2 tablespoons Irish cream liqueur
1 teaspoon ground cinnamon, divided
1 cup old-fashioned oats
6 tablespoons (¾ stick) cold butter, cut into pieces
⅔ cup packed brown sugar
¼ cup all-purpose flour
1 cup fresh blackberries
Irish Whipped Cream (recipe follows, optional)

1. Preheat oven to 375°F. Spray 9-inch oval or 8-inch square baking dish with nonstick cooking spray.

2. Place apples in large bowl; drizzle with lemon juice. Stir in granulated sugar, liqueur and ½ teaspoon cinnamon.

3. For topping, combine oats, butter, brown sugar, flour and remaining ½ teaspoon cinnamon in food processor; pulse until mixture is combined, leaving some some chunks remaining.

4. Gently stir blackberries into apple mixture. Pour into prepared baking dish; sprinkle with topping.

5. Bake 30 to 40 minutes or until filling is bubbly. Prepare Irish Whipped Cream, if desired. Serve with warm crisp. *Makes 6 servings*

IRISH WHIPPED CREAM: Beat 1 cup whipping cream and 2 tablespoons Irish cream liqueur in large bowl with electric mixer at high speed until slightly thickened. Add 1 to 2 tablespoons powdered sugar; beat until soft peaks form.

TRADITIONAL FRUIT CAKE

3 cups walnut halves

1 package (8 ounces) candied cherries

1 package (8 ounces) chopped dates

1 package (4 ounces) candied pineapple

¾ cup sifted all-purpose flour

¾ cup sugar

½ teaspoon baking powder

½ teaspoon salt

3 eggs, lightly beaten

3 tablespoons Irish whiskey or brandy

1 tablespoon grated orange peel

1 teaspoon vanilla

1. Preheat oven to 300°F. Line 9×5-inch loaf pan with parchment paper; spray with nonstick cooking spray.

2. Combine walnuts and fruit in large bowl. Sift flour, sugar, baking powder and salt into walnut mixture; toss gently to coat. Stir in eggs, whiskey, orange peel and vanilla until blended. Spread batter in prepared pan.

3. Bake 1 hour 45 minutes or until golden brown. Cool completely in pan on wire rack.

Makes 1 loaf

Gingerbread with Lemon Sauce

2½ cups all-purpose flour
1½ teaspoons ground cinnamon
1 teaspoon ground ginger
½ teaspoon baking soda
½ teaspoon salt
½ cup (1 stick) butter, softened
¾ cup packed brown sugar
⅓ cup light molasses
1 egg
¾ cup stout, at room temperature
Lemon Sauce (recipe follows)
Grated lemon peel (optional)

1. Preheat oven to 350°F. Spray 9-inch square baking pan with nonstick cooking spray.

2. Combine flour, cinnamon, ginger, baking soda and salt in medium bowl. Beat butter and brown sugar in large bowl with electric mixer at medium speed until light and fluffy. Add molasses and egg; beat until blended. Add flour mixture alternately with stout, beating until blended after each addition. Pour batter evenly into prepared pan.

3. Bake 35 to 40 minutes or until toothpick inserted into center comes out clean. Cool completely in pan on wire rack.

4. Prepare Lemon Sauce. Serve cake with sauce; sprinkle with lemon peel, if desired. *Makes 9 servings*

LEMON SAUCE: Combine 1 cup granulated sugar, ¾ cup whipping cream and ½ cup (1 stick) butter in small saucepan; cook and stir over medium heat until butter is melted. Reduce heat to low; simmer 5 minutes. Stir in 1 tablespoon lemon juice and 2 teaspoons grated lemon peel. Cool slightly.

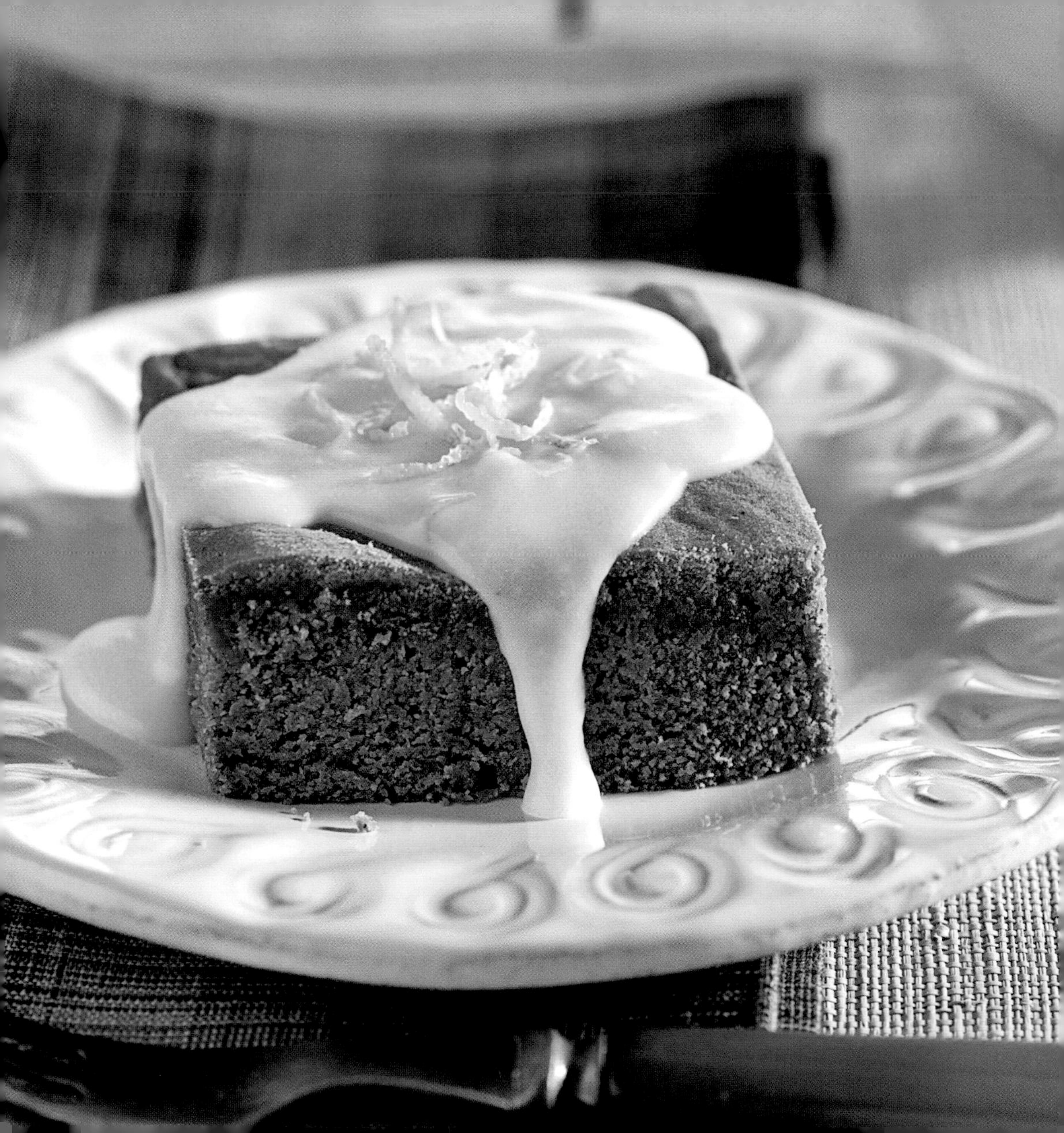

RUSTIC APPLE TART

Rustic Tart Dough (recipe follows)
2 pounds Golden Delicious apples, peeled and cut into ½-inch wedges
2 tablespoons lemon juice
½ cup plus 2 tablespoons sugar, divided
½ cup raisins
2½ tablespoons apple brandy or cognac, divided
1 teaspoon ground cinnamon
3 tablespoons butter, cut into pieces
1 cup apricot jam

1. Prepare Rustic Tart Dough.

2. Preheat oven to 400°F. Combine apples and lemon juice in large bowl. Add ½ cup sugar, raisins, 2 tablespoons brandy and cinnamon; toss to coat.

3. Cut piece of parchment paper to fit 15×10-inch jelly-roll pan. Place parchment on counter; sprinkle with flour. Place dough on parchment; sprinkle lightly with flour. Roll out dough into 18×16-inch oval about ¼ inch thick. Transfer parchment and dough to baking sheet.

4. Spread apple mixture over dough, leaving 2-inch border. Dot with butter. Fold edge of dough up and over filling, overlapping as necessary. Press gently to adhere to filling. Sprinkle edge of dough with remaining 2 tablespoons sugar.

5. Bake 50 to 55 minutes or until crust is browned and apples are tender. Cool slightly. Meanwhile, strain jam through sieve into small saucepan; cook and stir over low heat until smooth. Stir in remaining ½ tablespoon brandy. Brush warm tart with jam mixture. *Makes 8 servings*

RUSTIC TART DOUGH: Combine 2 cups all-purpose flour, 1 teaspoon sugar, 1 teaspoon grated lemon peel, ½ teaspoon salt and ½ teaspoon ground cinnamon in food processor; process until blended. Add ½ cup cold shortening; pulse until mixture forms pea-sized crumbs. Add ½ cup (1 stick) cold cubed butter; pulse until mixture resembles coarse crumbs. Add ⅓ cup ice water; process just until dough begins to come together. Shape dough into 6-inch disc; wrap with plastic wrap. Refrigerate at least 1 hour or overnight.

CHOCOLATE STOUT CAKE

2 cups all-purpose flour
¾ cup unsweetened cocoa powder
1 teaspoon baking soda
¼ teaspoon salt
1 cup packed brown sugar
¾ cup (1½ sticks) butter, softened
½ cup granulated sugar
1 teaspoon vanilla
3 eggs
1 cup stout, at room temperature
   Cream Cheese Frosting (recipe follows)

1. Preheat oven to 350°F. Spray 13×9-inch baking pan with nonstick cooking spray.

2. Combine flour, cocoa, baking soda and salt in medium bowl. Beat brown sugar, butter and granulated sugar in large bowl with electric mixer at medium speed until light and fluffy. Beat in vanilla. Add eggs, one at a time, beating well after each addition. Add flour mixture alternately with stout, beating until blended after each addition. Pour batter evenly into prepared pan.

3. Bake 35 to 40 minutes or until toothpick inserted into center comes out clean. Cool completely in pan on wire rack.

4. Prepare Cream Cheese Frosting. Spread frosting over cake.

Makes 12 servings

CREAM CHEESE FROSTING: Beat 1 package (8 ounces) softened cream cheese and ¼ cup (½ stick) softened butter in large bowl with electric mixer at medium speed until creamy. Gradually beat in 4 cups powdered sugar and vanilla until smooth. Add 1 tablespoon milk; beat until smooth. Beat in additional 1 to 2 tablespoons milk, if necessary, to reach spreading consistency.

MOLDED SHORTBREAD

1½ cups all-purpose flour
¼ teaspoon salt
¾ cup (1½ sticks) butter, softened
⅓ cup sugar
1 egg

1. Preheat oven to temperature recommended by shortbread mold manufacturer. Spray 10-inch ceramic shortbread mold with nonstick cooking spray.

2. Combine flour and salt in medium bowl. Beat butter and sugar in large bowl with electric mixer at medium speed until light and fluffy. Add egg; beat until well blended. Gradually add flour mixture; beat at low speed until blended. Press dough firmly into mold.

3. Bake, cool and remove shortbread from mold according to manufacturer's directions. *Makes 1 shortbread mold*

NOTE: If shortbread mold is not available, preheat oven to 350°F. Shape dough into 1-inch balls. Place 2 inches apart on ungreased cookie sheets; press with fork to flatten. Bake 18 to 20 minutes or until edges are lightly browned. Cool cookies on cookie sheets 2 minutes; remove to wire racks to cool completely. Makes 2 dozen cookies.

APPLE CAKE

4 medium apples, cut into ¼-inch slices (4 cups)
Juice of ½ lemon
1 cup sugar
3 cups all-purpose flour
¾ cup chopped almonds
1½ teaspoons baking soda
1 teaspoon ground cinnamon
½ teaspoon salt
½ teaspoon ground nutmeg
1 cup vegetable oil
1 teaspoon vanilla

1. Preheat oven to 350°F. Spray 13×9-inch baking pan with nonstick cooking spray.

2. Place apple slices in medium bowl. Drizzle with lemon juice and sprinkle with sugar; toss to coat. Let stand 20 minutes or until juice forms.

3. Combine flour, almonds, baking soda, cinnamon, salt and nutmeg in large bowl. Add oil and vanilla; stir until well blended. Stir in apple mixture. Spread batter in prepared pan.

4. Bake about 35 minutes or until browned and toothpick inserted into center comes out clean. Cool in pan on wire rack 10 minutes. Serve warm.

Makes 16 servings

NOTE: Either whole skin-on almonds or sliced almonds can be used.

LEMON CURD

6 tablespoons butter
1 cup sugar
6 tablespoons lemon juice
2 teaspoons grated lemon peel
3 eggs, lightly beaten

1. Melt butter in double boiler set over simmering water. Stir in sugar, lemon juice and lemon peel.

2. Stir in eggs until blended. Cook and stir 15 to 20 minutes over low heat or until mixture is thick and smooth.

3. Remove from heat; let cool. (Curd will thicken as it cools.) Cover and refrigerate 2 hours or until cold. Serve chilled. Store in refrigerator up to 3 weeks. *Makes 1¾ cups*

POACHED DRIED FRUIT COMPOTE

1½ cups water
8 ounces mixed dried fruit, such as apricots, pears, apples and prunes
½ cup Riesling or other white wine
2 cinnamon sticks
4 whole cloves

1. Combine water, dried fruit, wine, cinnamon sticks and cloves in medium saucepan; bring to a boil over high heat. Reduce heat to low; simmer, uncovered, 12 to 15 minutes or until fruit is tender.

2. Cool slightly. Discard cinnamon sticks and cloves. Serve warm, at room temperature or chilled. *Makes 6 servings*

ACKNOWLEDGMENTS

The publisher would like to thank the companies and organizations listed below
for the use of their recipes and photographs in this publication.

American Lamb Board

Cabot® Creamery Cooperative

Campbell Soup Company

Filippo Berio® Olive Oil

Reckitt Benckiser LLC

The Quaker® Oatmeal Kitchens

INDEX

METRIC CONVERSION CHART

VOLUME MEASUREMENTS (dry)

$1/8$ teaspoon = 0.5 mL
$1/4$ teaspoon = 1 mL
$1/2$ teaspoon = 2 mL
$3/4$ teaspoon = 4 mL
1 teaspoon = 5 mL
1 tablespoon = 15 mL
2 tablespoons = 30 mL
$1/4$ cup = 60 mL
$1/3$ cup = 75 mL
$1/2$ cup = 125 mL
$2/3$ cup = 150 mL
$3/4$ cup = 175 mL
1 cup = 250 mL
2 cups = 1 pint = 500 mL
3 cups = 750 mL
4 cups = 1 quart = 1 L

VOLUME MEASUREMENTS (fluid)

1 fluid ounce (2 tablespoons) = 30 mL
4 fluid ounces ($1/2$ cup) = 125 mL
8 fluid ounces (1 cup) = 250 mL
12 fluid ounces ($1 1/2$ cups) = 375 mL
16 fluid ounces (2 cups) = 500 mL

WEIGHTS (mass)

$1/2$ ounce = 15 g
1 ounce = 30 g
3 ounces = 90 g
4 ounces = 120 g
8 ounces = 225 g
10 ounces = 285 g
12 ounces = 360 g
16 ounces = 1 pound = 450 g

DIMENSIONS

$1/16$ inch = 2 mm
$1/8$ inch = 3 mm
$1/4$ inch = 6 mm
$1/2$ inch = 1.5 cm
$3/4$ inch = 2 cm
1 inch = 2.5 cm

OVEN TEMPERATURES

250°F = 120°C
275°F = 140°C
300°F = 150°C
325°F = 160°C
350°F = 180°C
375°F = 190°C
400°F = 200°C
425°F = 220°C
450°F = 230°C

BAKING PAN AND DISH EQUIVALENTS

Utensil	Size in Inches	Size in Centimeters	Volume	Metric Volume
Baking or Cake	8×8×2	20×20×5	8 cups	2 L
Pan (square or	9×9×2	23×23×5	10 cups	2.5 L
rectangular)	13×9×2	33×23×5	12 cups	3 L
Loaf Pan	8½×4½×2½	21×11×6	6 cups	1.5 L
	9×9×3	23×13×7	8 cups	2 L
Round Layer	8×1½	20×4	4 cups	1 L
Cake Pan	9×1½	23×4	5 cups	1.25 L
Pie Plate	8×1½	20×4	4 cups	1 L
	9×1½	23×4	5 cups	1.25 L
Baking Dish or			1 quart/4 cups	1 L
Casserole			1½ quart/6 cups	1.5 L
			2 quart/8 cups	2 L
			3 quart/12 cups	3 L